THE YACHTSMAN'S QUIZ BOOK

THE YACHTSMAN'S QUIZ BOOK

Martin Muncaster

DAVID & CHARLES
Newton Abbot   London

British Library Cataloguing in Publication Data

Muncaster, Martin
   The Yachtsman's Quiz Book
   1. Seafaring life – Miscellanea
   I. Title
   910.4′ 5   G540

   ISBN 0-7153-8291-8

Typeset by Typesetters (Birmingham) Limited,
Edgbaston Road, Smethwick, Warley, West Midlands
and printed in Great Britain
by A. Wheaton & Co., Hennock Road, Exeter
for David & Charles (Publishers) Limited
Brunel House   Newton Abbot   Devon

Contents

Introduction

This is not a quiz aimed at the professionals. Anyone in the marine business should attain high marks without difficulty. I have compiled this little quiz more for those with a less professional involvement with the maritime world, and especially for the average yachtsman who goes down to the sea in his boat for pleasure; who takes to the waters around our coasts and beyond to find relief from the pains and pressures of our headlong world. What yachtsman, or yachtswoman, does not absorb therapy from the sing of the wind in the rigging or that magical sound of water frothing past the bow of their boat as she creams her way to landfall? But that's the romance. There are plenty of frights and spills, too, specially for the racing fraternity who tend to take more risks than we crusty cruising folk.

Be that as it may, this particular cruising sailor has found fun in the writing of this book and I've learned a lot! It has been a challenge and has certainly had the effect of working up a thirst for knowledge.

The sea, and all things pertaining thereto, encompasses a vast range of subject, of course, and it would take several tomes to cover it all. But I hope I have achieved a book that offers something of interest to most – some reasonably easy questions, some testing ones. I am all too well aware that definitions have developed via generations of seafarers and their widely differing vessels, that the lore of the sea is evolving all the time and that there can be, therefore, debate about the validity of a particular answer. I can only say that I have done my best to avoid ambiguities and have worked from sources of proven reliability.

I am indebted to many people for their help in the compilation of the quiz, but I would especially like to thank the following who have taken endless trouble on my behalf, particularly in the navigational, Royal Navy, historical and racing chapters:

Gus Britton; Rear Admiral P. W. Brock, CB, DSO; John Coleman; Commander Richard Compton-Hall, MBE, RN (Ret'd); Martin Everard; John Glover Wyllie; Peter Nunn; Captain Michael Ortmans, MVO, RN; Jeremy Pallant; Lord Riverdale ARINA, ex-Commodore of the Royal Cruising Club; and Captain John Williams.

My thanks are also due particularly to the librarians of the College of Nautical Studies, Warsash, and the Royal Naval Submarine Museum at HMS *Dolphin*, Gosport; to Richard Baker and Michael Fish for their very kind assistance with the music and weather chapters; and to Keith Shackleton for his invaluable help with the questions on birds.

The figure in question 47 on page 14 is based on an illustration in Eric Hiscock's *Cruising Under Sail* (2nd ed, OUP), and that in question 48 is based on an illustration on page 236 of *A Dictionary of Sailing* by F. H. Burgess (Penguin Reference Books, 1961. © F. H. Burgess 1961).

I do hope the reader will have as much fun in tackling the quiz as I have had in putting it together.

Martin Muncaster, 1982

I

A Question of Seamanship

Sailing

1 From which direction is the wind coming when one is
  sailing on a:
  (a) close reach?
  (b) beam reach?
  (c) broad reach?
2 If a sailing vessel is 'hove-to', how are the sails and helm set?
3 What is meant by 'lee bowing'?
4 When is a yacht said to be 'ghosting'?
5 When moving about the boat, what is the seafarer's time-
  honoured rule for personal safety?
6 These illustrations show a halyard made up on a cleat. In
  which one is the rope correctly made up?

1   2   3

7 A sailor might well take a swig of rum; how else will he use
  the word 'swig'?

8 If you wish to get more efficiency out of your sails, how will a 'Cunningham' help you?
9 On which side of the mainsail should you stand when reefing?
10 From the illustration, how would you describe your yacht's point of sailing?

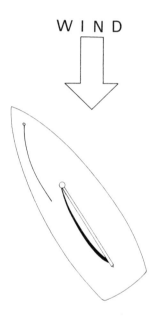

11 There is a vertical line marked on the inside of the mariner's compass bowl indicating the direction in which the ship's head lies. What is this line called?
12 If you were asked to 'box the compass', what would you do?
13 What is the 'kingspoke'?
14 On studying the chart you observe that your ship's course will take you across an area marked thus: ✳

What are you being warned about?
15 You are going well under full sail, but notice a line of dark cloud approaching, beneath which is a long streak of white foam on the water. What is likely to happen very shortly and what should you be doing about it?

16 Night has closed in while on passage and you see ahead the lights shown in the illustration:

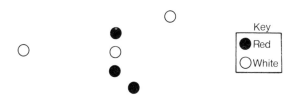

What do they tell you?

17 Sailing at night with the true wind abeam to port you see a single green light on a steady bearing about 4 points on the port bow. What is it, and what action should you take?

18 'Telltales' are short lengths of wool attached to sails or rigging to enable the helmsman to determine the flow of wind and thereby set his sails to best advantage. What is another use for the term?

19 What is meant by the term 'top hamper'?

20 When navigating a boat, the effect of the tidal stream has to be taken carefully into consideration. What is the difference between 'set' and 'drift'?

21 When a yacht is said to be sailing 'full and bye', what is meant?

22 'Green to green – red to red . . .' Can you complete this old 'rule of the road' mnemonic?

23 A single fixed white light at sea can mean a number of different things. What are they?

24 Checking your chart as you plan a cruise, you see the following symbols at different points along the track you mean to take:

(a) 5 kn

(b) 1 kn

What do they mean?

25 By day, the wind drops considerably as you sail towards your destination and you decide to motor-sail to help your craft make progress over a strong tide. What signal should you hoist to indicate that you are now a vessel under sail and power?

26 When is a rudder said to be balanced?

27 The barometer can give information of value to the seaman on matters concerning the weather. In tidal waters, what else could it tell him?

28 A yacht is entering a strange harbour by day under motor. Her skipper, expecting to pick up a mooring, or tie up alongside, makes the following preparations: he has ready sufficient warps and fenders for either side of the vessel, and a megaphone; he makes the dinghy ready, with oars and crutches prepared and a boathook to hand. Should he prepare anything else?

29 Sailing on a day of sunshine and showers, you see a rainbow. A beautiful sight, but can you name the colours and the order in which they appear?

30 From his single mooring in a fresh wind, but no tide, a yachtsman decides to get away to starboard. He hoists the mainsail and the jib, both loosely sheeted, and as he casts off he backs the jib to port. What else can he do to assist his departure?

Sails and Sailmaking

Sails

31 A small jib, often made of canvas, is used in heavy weather. What is it called?

32 Sailors have been known to tie a figure of eight knot in a headsail to reduce its size. What is the result called?

33 What is a 'balloon' jib?

34 What is a 'raffee sail'?

35 What is a 'stuns'l' (or studdingsail)?

36 What is a ringtail?

37 What is a 'bonnet'?

38 A mizzen sail on a ketch or yawl may be named a . . .?

39 If you 'dowse' a sail, what do you do to it?

40 If you 'scandalise' a sail what do you do to it?

Sailmaking

41 When a sailmaker makes a sail, on which side does he sew the bolt rope?

42 What is the 'tabling' on a sail?

43 What is 'herring-boning'?

44 Wherabouts is the roach of a sail in:
   (a) a square sail?
   (b) a fore-and-aft sail?

Rig

45 How would you describe this type of sail?

46 Can you give the names of the various parts of a gaff rig?

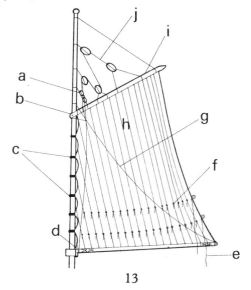

47 Silhouettes of rigs. Can you name them?

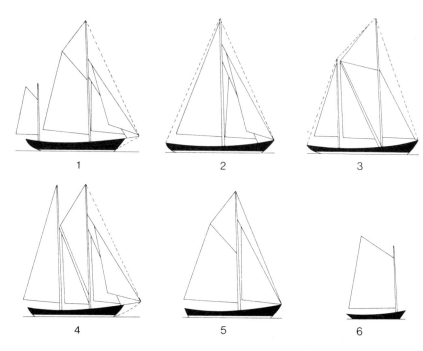

1   2   3

4   5   6

48 Can you name the various sails on this square rigger?

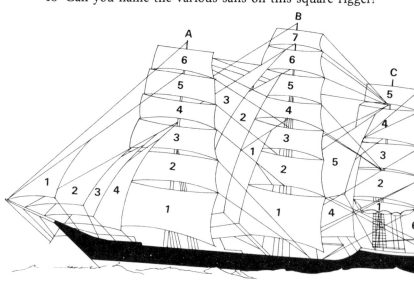

What Is and What Are?

Gear

49 What is a 'deadeye'?

50 What is a fid?

51 What is a 'fiddle block'?

52 What is a jigger, or handy billy?

53 What is a sweep (other than a 'sweep' for mines)?

54 What is a tack tackle (usually pronounced 'taikle')?

55 What is a whisker pole?

56 'Pudding' (or 'puddening') on a vessel is nothing to do with the sweet course of a good lunch. What is it?

57 Most people call them rowlocks. What is their proper name?

58 What, in fact, are rowlocks?

Parts of Ship

59 What is a 'booby hatch'?

60 What is a dolphin striker?

61 What is a fife rail?

62 What is the name for the metal band which clamps the inboard end of a bowsprit to the deck?

63 What is a jib-boom as opposed to a bowsprit?

64 Describe a lee board.

65 What is a 'martingale'?

66 What is the name for the sliding loop, or rope which holds a yard to the mast and enables it to be hoisted or lowered as required?

67 What is the sheer strake?

68 These are pins fixed upright onto the gunwales of a rowing boat which act in the same manner as rowlocks. What are they called?

Construction

69 What is the name for the wooden or perspex screen round the bridge of a ship or, in sailing yachts, the canvas screens rigged at the sides of the cockpit?

70 What is the 'escutcheon' of a vessel?

71 The first row of planks or plates next to the keel has a particular name. What is it?

72 What is the 'king plank'?

73 What is an alternative name for 'clinker built' boats?

74 What is a 'mould loft'?

75 What is a reaming iron?

76 Can you give the term employed to describe the short insert of planking used to fill in where a plank falls short of the required length?

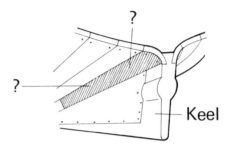

77 In this boat's transom what is the name given to the timbers marked?

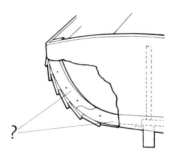

78 How would you describe these hull shapes?

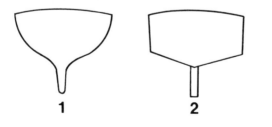

Anchoring

79 Can you name these types of anchor?

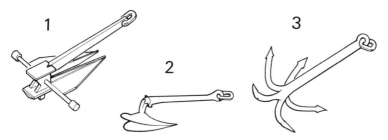

80 What is the name for this type of anchor? Can you list the various parts?

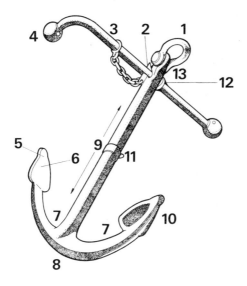

81 Choosing a safe anchorage can be difficult. Give ten main aspects to be considered when anchoring your vessel.

82 Large ships carry two main anchors and a further spare anchor for use in emergency.
   (a) What are the main anchors called?
   (b) How are they stowed?
   (c) What is the spare anchor called?

83 What are the following?
  (a) A 'scotchman'.
  (b) A navel or spurling pipe.
  (c) A gypsy.
  (d) A tripping line.
84 What is a kedge anchor normally used for in a yacht?
85 When the anchor is being raised, what is the cry from the foredeck when the anchor leaves the bottom?

Three in One

Can you think of one word which will describe all three items in the following groups?

86 (a) A mooring post ashore for securing a vessel.
  (b) A permanent fender around the gunwale of a heavy boat to prevent chafe or damage to other boats.
  (c) A fish, or more correctly, a mammal.
87 (a) To come up into wind despite the pressure of the helm.
  (b) The curved portion of a vessel's stem which cleaves the water as she moves ahead.
  (c) A canvas lashing or steel hook used to secure a seaboat or lifeboat in the davits.
88 (a) The leading edge of a sail.
  (b) To bring the boat's head up into the wind.
  (c) A 'purchase' consisting of a single or double block which can be used for hauling to better advantage.
89 (a) The lower fore corner of a sail.
  (b) To change the course of a sailing boat by bringing her head up to or through the wind.
  (c) Weevils usually fall out of this!
90 (a) Bubbly.
  (b) Grog.
  (c) Nelson's blood.
91 (a) A piece of timber or iron fitted to the lower edge of a rudder to even it up to the false keel (the additional keel added to the after part of the main keel for protection or rudder attachment).
  (b) The cabin or cockpit deck.
  (c) The foundation plate for the support of an inboard engine.

Knotty Problems

Knots and Not Knots

92 Can you name the knots, bends and hitches illustrated on this and the following page?

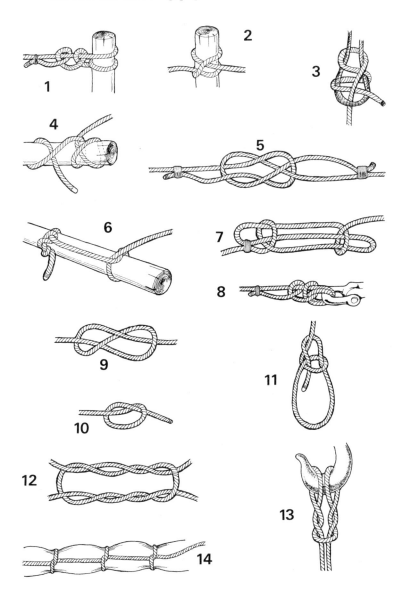

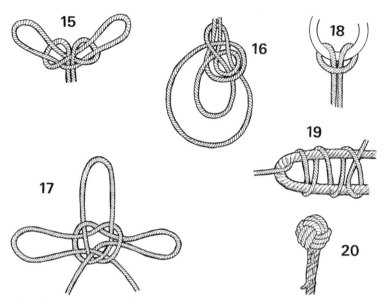

93 Give some uses for the knots in the previous question.
94 What is the difference between a bend and a hitch? Are they both knots?
95 What is the best way to loosen a tightly shrunken bend, hitch or knot?
96 What has been done to this hook?

Rope
97 (a) What are the two names given to the rough rope made from the outer husk of the coconut?
   (b) What are its disadvantages?
   (c) It does have advantages, however. What are they?

98 What is sisal made from and where is it cultivated?
99 (a) What is a French flake?
  (b) Can you give the two terms used to describe the way of coiling a rope on deck as shown in the illustration?
  (c) When should a rope not be coiled in this way and why not?

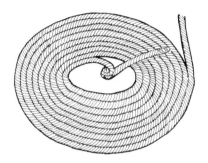

100 The words 'worming', 'parcelling' and 'serving' go together. What is their significance to a piece of rope?
101 What is the 'fall' of a rope?
102 What is a gantline?
103 What is marline?
104 What is oakum and what is it used for?

A Sailor's Forecasting

General
105 (a) Was the Meteorological Office first instituted in 1684, 1854 or 1954?
  (b) Under which government department did it come at the time?
106 What is the difference between a barometer and a barograph?
107 Give a definition of isobars.
108 Do winds at sea blow exactly parallel to the isobars, or are they deflected? If so, by how much?
109 What hazard would you expect to find in a tropical maritime air mass, eg mild south-westerly winds when the sea is cold?
110 What is a 'willy-willy'?

111 If you hear warnings of gales as (a) imminent, (b) soon, (c) later, when would you expect them?

112 At what height are winds measured at meteorological stations around the world?

113 What do the following weather symbols mean?

₁∇ ₂⌐⟨ ₃≡ ₄● ₅✳ ₆❜

114 Can a low of, say, 1016 Mb as well as a high of 1016 Mb appear on the same chart, and if so, does the weather differ?

Come Wind and Weather

115 In the Northern Hemisphere, what is a basic method of determining where low pressure lies? And the law's name?

116 What is a geostrophic wind?

117 What gives rise to coastal slope winds?

118 Katabatic winds blow downhill, particularly at night. What is the term used to describe the lift of air created by hills warmed by the morning sun?

119 What type of wind accompanies thunderstorms and heavy showers?

120 In what year was wind speed first drawn up in a scale for seamen?

121 Give the name of the admiral who invented the scale.

122 He has become famous for his wind scale, but what else was he noted for?

123 'Small trees in leaf sway. Tops of tall trees in noticeable motion . . .' describes which wind force?

124 What is the phrase used to describe this force, and what are its limits of wind speed in knots?

125 What does Force 12 in the scale denote?

126 Can you name the forecast areas shown blank opposite?

Winds of the World

127 Sailors at sea in the Gulf of Lions, particularly during winter, have to beware of a certain cold wind that can spring up suddenly and violently.
 (a) What is it called?
 (b) How is its name derived?
 (c) Where is the Gulf of Lions?

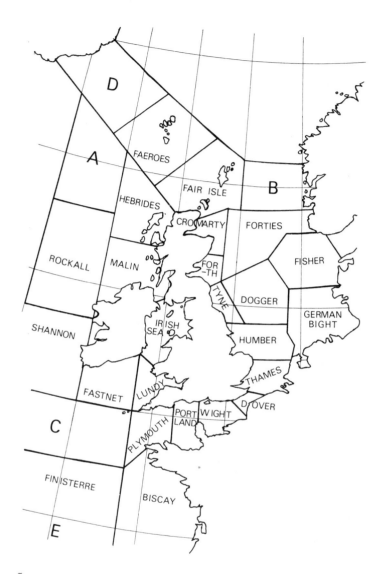

128 A hot, dust laden southerly wind which blows from the Libyan Desert across the Mediterranean also has a name. What is it?

129 Hot winds originating in other dry, heated regions also have their own particular names, eg the Khamsin of Egypt. What is the one for Spain?

130 Where would you find a 'Pampero'?

Clouds

131 These abbreviations describe various cloud types; what are
they?

   (a) Cu.   (f) Cb.

   (b) As.   (g) Cc.

   (c) St.   (h) Sc.

   (d) Cs.   (i) Ns.

   (e) Ac.   (j) Ci.

132 What is the connection between thunder and a blacksmith?

133 What type of cloud is sometimes called 'cauliflower cloud'?

134 If you saw high Ci cloud streaming out in parallel lines or
banners across the sky, what sort of weather would you
expect to follow?

135 When he is experiencing low, scudding cloud, the sailor
usually calls the cloud 'scud'. Can you give its proper name?

136 Describe the following:

   (a) depression (low).

   (b) occlusion.

137 What is happening when a 'trough' is said to be filling?

138 How can the Azores High affect our summer weather for
the better, particularly in southern Britain?

Can you Complete?

139 Long foretold, long last, . . .

140 When the glass falls low, . . .
When it slowly rises high, . . .

141 At sea with low and falling glass,
Soundly sleeps . . .

142 A red sky at night . . .
A red sky . . .

143 Mackerel sky and mares' tails, . . .

144 When the wind shifts against the sun
Trust it not . . .

145 First (or sharp) rise after blow . . .

146 If clouds are gathering thick and fast,
Keep sharp lookout for sail and mast.
But if they slowly onward crawl, . . .

2

Navigation

The Practice of Navigation

1 You have heard of the three 'R's in education; by a similar old maxim, what are the three 'L's in navigation?

2 When making a landfall what is meant by 'aiming off'?

3 How would you use a single LOP to locate a small island when uncertain of your own position?

4 In general, what is the best time of day to approach a strange coast?

5 How would you adjust the ship's clock when bound from Panama to New Zealand? Would you adjust the ship's chronometer at the same time?

6 How many methods can you think of for checking the deviation of the compass?

7 If you find it necessary to transfer the position of a rock from one chart to another of the same area, how should this be done?

8 How would you assess the reliability of a chart?

9 What is a rising or dipping light and how would you make use of such an observation?

10 What is the method recommended for navigating through an area of coral reefs?

Tools of the Trade

11 How many types of ship's log can you think of and what does each log measure?

12 The ship's binnacle may contain up to five different types of correctors. Can you name these and describe the functions they perform?

13 What is integral and derivative control on an auto pilot?

14 What is the cause of latitude course and speed error in a gyro compass?

15 What precautions would you take when using an echo sounder with phasing facilities?

16 The chart of the Red Sea states that depths measured by echo sounder should be increased by 5 per cent. Why is this?

17 How does a rhumb line appear on:
(a) a Mercator chart?
(b) a gnomonic chart?

18 Why does radio direction finding tend to be unreliable at dawn, dusk and throughout the night?

19 Having calibrated a ship's DF on 300kHz, why should it be necessary to take check bearings on 500kHz?

20 How do the following errors arise on a marine sextant?
(a) Perpendicularity.
(b) Side error.
(c) Index error.

Nautical Astronomy

21 How would you locate the Pole Star and what is significant about the true altitude of the Pole Star?

22 What is a circumpolar star and in what latitude would Alioth (declination 56°N) be just circumpolar?

23 Name the individual corrections to an altitude of the sun's upper or lower limb.

24 What is the brightest star in the night sky? From which constellation does it come and how would you locate it?

25 Name the four navigational planets. Why is the 'v' correction for Venus sometimes negative?

26 What is the Equation of Time?

27 Why do the values of SHA and declination for the selected stars in the *Nautical Almanac* experience a gradual change?

28 What is a lunation?

29 When planning star sights would you use civil twilight or nautical twilight?

30 In latitude 50°N you watched the sun rise bearing 090°T; what was its declination?

Electronic Aids

31 How should an octohedral radar reflector be correctly hoisted?

32 What is a racon?

33 The fairway buoy towards which you are running, can be seen dead ahead, but on the radar screen it appears 3° to starboard of the heading marker. What is the reason for this apparent discrepancy?

34 In a hyperbolic navigation system what is meant by 'lane expansion', and why is it small in the Omega system and large in the Decca Navigator system?

35 Why does the Transit Satellite transmit on two frequencies?

36 How is 'sky wave effect' eliminated in the Loran C system?

37 How many modes of radar display can you think of?

38 Why do the stations in a Decca chain transmit on different frequencies and how are they compared in the receiver?

39 What is doppler radar?

40 What do the following abbreviations stand for?

(a) PPI.   (d) CECS.

(b) ARPA.   (e) LOP.

(c) SID.   (f) SINS.

3
Racing

Around the Marks

1 You sail over the start line in a very light wind when the 5 minute gun goes. The wind drops and you discover the tide is taking you back towards the line. You throw an anchor over and drop back across the line on a warp. The crew on a boat nearby shout 'protest'. Are they right?

2 You have started 4 seconds early in front of a group of boats which now hinder your return to re-start. At what point do you lose all rights over the following boats?

3 Having started early you go back across the line and immediately round onto the starboard tack catching a late starter coming up on port tack with the port hand starting line buoy just under his lee. Much to his consternation you shout 'Starboard' and carry on. Are you right?

4 You are about to re-start after a general recall. In the hurly-burly you have lost track of the exact time of the start. You expect a gun as a starting signal but a hooter sounds, the 'I' flag is raised and the 5 and 10 minute flags are lowered. What does the 'I' flag signify and do you start now?

5 You are close-hauled on port tack when you misjudge an opponent's speed when he is on starboard and just clip his stern. He shouts 'Gyrate' and you agree to make two 360° turns. After completing the first turn another competitor on port tack asks for water. 'Forget him and let's get on with it' says your crew. Is he right?

6 You are sailing close-hauled for the windward mark. Under the racing rules when are you luffing and when are you tacking?

7 You are close-hauled on starboard tack and approaching another competitor who is on port tack. He decides to go

about in order to miss you, at which point you decide to go on to port tack. He shouts angrily that you should have called starboard. Did you need to?

8 You are beating close inshore on port tack and about to go aground. Outside you and on collision course with you, are two boats on starboard tack. Both these shout 'Starboard' at you. Is there anything you can do about it?

9 You are on starboard tack and about to round a mark at the end of a windward leg. A competitor is sailing up to the mark on port tack and calls for water to round inside you. Do you need to give him room?

10 You are sailing an offwind leg of the course on port tack in open water. An overtaking boat on starboard comes up from astern and shouts for you to get out of his way. Do you need to?

11 On a blustery day you are approaching the finishing line well ahead of your rivals when you capsize. 'Come on,' shouts your crew, 'let's swim her across.' 'No', you say, 'we'll have to let the tide carry us across.' Is either of you right?

12 You are racing level with a competitor towards the finishing line when he lets his spinnaker flap forward over the line. 'I'm first across', he shouts. Is he right?

The America's Cup

13 Where and when did the first America's Cup race take place?

14 What was the original trophy called and why was it subsequently called the America's Cup?

15 Why did the British dispute *America*'s victory?

16 Who is reported to have received the reply: 'There is no second . . .'?

17 Where is the America's Cup kept?

18 What, is it said, will replace it, if the Cup is ever lost?

19 How many America's Cup matches have there been?

20 In all these, how many races has the USA lost? And won?

21 Who was known as 'Tea-pot Tommy' and what is his connection with the America's Cup?

22 Since 1930, the races have been held off Newport, Rhode Island. Who has been the most successful challenger in these waters?

23 Why do some argue that the race should have gone the other way?

24 What headline appeared in an American newspaper after this event?

25 Since 1958, the races have been between 12-metre yachts. What is the formula for a '12-metre'?

26 Which well known naturalist helmed a British challenger?

27 Which helmsman was replaced and by whom, on board *Lionheart* in 1980?

28 Who was the winning helmsman, and what was the name of the winning yacht in 1980?

29 Who was the losing helmsman, and what was the name of the losing yacht that year?

30 What design feature, copied from *Lionheart* could have tipped the scales in the Australians' favour?

31 What trophy is awarded to the losing challenger and where is it kept?

32 How many yachts have defended the America's Cup more than once? What were their names, and who did they beat and when?

Racing and Cruising Milestones

33 When did the first recorded yacht race take place in England, and where?

34 Which is the oldest design of British keel boat still racing?

35 Which was the first centreboard dinghy class to be raced regularly internationally?

36 Who has been the only man to win a first-class dinghy championship in the same class a dozen times?

37 Who captained Britain's victorious Admiral's Cup team in 1971?

38 Who designed the immensely successful *Flying Fifteen*?

39 Who wrote of Captain Joshua Slocum: 'his place in history is as secure as Adam's'?

40 When was the first international speed-boat race held?

41 When was the first Fastnet Race and which yacht won it?

42 What was significant about the sloop *April Fool*?

43 Who was the first man to voyage single-handed round the world without any port of call?

44 Who was the first woman to sail across an ocean alone and how did it come about?

45 Who was the first man to put forward the idea of a single-handed sailing race?

46 Who won the Observer Europe 1 Two-handed Race across the Atlantic in 1981?

47 How did Maurice and Maralyn Bailey make history?

4

The Queen's Navee

Great Sea Battles and Ships

Battles

1 Why did a duke set sail from the mouth of the Somme one September night to cross the Channel?

2 Who spoke this famous prayer and on the occasion of what action? What did the action achieve?

> O Lord God when thou givest to thy servants to endeavour any great matter, grant us also to know that it is not the beginning, but the continuing of the same, until it be thoroughly finished, which yieldeth the true glory; through Him that for the finishing of thy work laid down his life, our Redeemer, Jesus Christ. Amen.

3 Who, after a battle in 1798, became 'Duke of Bronté'?

4 Can you arrange these battles in their chronological order: The Saints; Kentish Knock; The Glorious First of June; Solebay; Quiberon Bay; The North Cape?

5 What British coin links the year 1346, the Battle of 'Les Espanols sur Mer' in 1350 and a Jutland casualty in 1916?

6 In which famous naval battle did the author of *Don Quixote* fight?

7 What naval battle virtually decided the loss of the American colonies?

8 Apart from his *Bounty* fame, Captain Bligh commanded ships at two famous battles. Can you name these?

9 Where did a combined fleet of British, French and Russian ships defeat a fleet of Egyptian and Turkish ships?

10 In 1942, British ships lying in Alexandria Harbour experienced not just an unhappy Christmas, more a disastrous one. What happened?

11 Name the only battleship to be sunk by an air to surface missile.

12 What were the following?
   (a) Operation Neptune.
   (b) Operation Dynamo.
   (c) Operation Husky.
   (d) Operation Source.
   (e) Operation Torch.
   (f) Operation Sealion.
   (g) Operation Weserübung.
   (h) Operation Frankton.
   (i) Operation Jubilee.
   (j) Operation Pedestal.

Ships

13 What is the oldest warship still afloat?

14 The first *Dreadnought* fought against the Spanish Armada. Which ship is the latest to hold the name and when was she launched?

15 Can you answer the following questions on HMS *Ark Royal*?
   (a) What was the first *Ark Royal*'s claim to fame?
   (b) What was her original name?
   (c) A television series made the most recent *Ark Royal* (the aircraft carrier) famous. What was the fate of her predecessor?
   (d) Who sang the theme song for the TV series and what was the song called?
   (e) The following battle honours, except one, were among those gained by ships bearing the name *Ark Royal*: Armada, 1588; Trafalgar, 1805; Dardanelles, 1915; Norway, 1940; Malta Convoys, 1941; Spartivento, 1940. Which is the odd one out?
   (f) What famous German warship's name features in *Ark Royal*'s battle honours?

16 What was unusual about the *Charlotte Dundas*, launched before Trafalgar?

17 On the night of 22 October 1707, a famous British admiral, after successful operations in the Mediterranean, suffered shipwreck off a cluster of islands. The admiral, on his way home for the winter, went down with his flagship. Three

other ships foundered also with the loss of some eight hundred officers and men.

(a) Who was the admiral?

(b) Can you name the islands where he came to grief?

(c) What was the name of his ship?

18 In the reign of Queen Victoria the Admiralty organised an experimental tug of war between a paddle driven and a screw driven tug to decide which was the better method of propulsion. What were their names and which one won the contest?

19 What ship, a veteran of the Battle of Jutland, is still afloat today?

20 At the start of World War II, at 6pm on 17 September 1939, the Royal Navy lost its first capital ship to enemy action. Who was she and how was she sunk?

21 This famous German pocket battleship was named after the admiral who was victor of the Battle of Coronel in 1914. She sank a dozen merchant ships in the South Atlantic in October and November 1939 and was eventually tracked down by three British ships off the mouth of a great river.

(a) What was the ship's name?

(b) Which was the river in the question?

(c) Can you name the three British ships which attacked the German battleship?

22 In World War II the town class cruiser, HMS *Belfast*, had a twin sister. Who was she and where is she now?

23 In the winter of 1940 this German pocket battleship patrolling the Atlantic, sighted a convoy of thirty-seven Allied ships escorted only by an armed merchant cruiser. The captain of the British warship signalled the convoy to scatter while he steamed out alone to challenge the enemy. This British warship eventually went down in the action; however, all but five of the merchantmen escaped. What was the name of the German battleship, and what was the name of the British armed merchant cruiser?

24 What was the name of the ship allegedly within sight of the *Titanic* when she went down in 1912 after striking an iceberg?

Flags and Signals

The Royal Yacht

25 Who is now the Lord High Admiral?

26 When HM the Queen is afloat in the Royal Yacht in UK waters, what flags are worn at the mastheads?

27 When the Royal Yacht is dressed overall, what happens to the dressing flags rigged between the foremast and mainmast when the ship is 'undressed'?

28 When does the Royal Yacht fly the white ensign on her ensign staff?

29 Why do Royal Yacht Officers not wear the link button in the jacket of their mess undress?

30 For how long can a rating remain in the Yacht service?

31 What is the rank of the commanding officer?

32 When were the crew first allowed to drink beer on board the Yacht when at sea?

33 What is the difference between the trousers of a normal naval rating and a Royal Yacht rating when square rig is being worn?

34 Admirals are piped on board ships flying the white ensign; when is the Flag Officer Royal Yachts piped on board the ship which he commands?

35 With royalty on board, when do officers and men remove their caps when walking on the upper deck?

36 Why was the Yacht built with a garage?

Naval Tradition

37 At what point is the Union flag lowered from the jackstaff of a warship when she is leaving harbour?

38 Who on a ship would be 'Sticks'?

39 At what time is the white ensign hauled down at sea?

40 Legend has it that years ago when a warship came to the end of her commission, the ship's company knotted together all their brightwork cleaning rags and hoisted them to fly from the main truck as a 'paying off' pendant. What does a ship's 'paying off' pendant look like today?

41 What is a single green and white pendant customarily called?

42 Who is known as 'Flags' in the Royal Navy?

43 When are 'sixteen bells' struck in the Royal Navy?

44 Who traditionally has the duty of striking the sixteen bells and what is he nicknamed?
45 Why is whistling prohibited in HM ships?
46 Who is the only rating in the Royal Navy permitted to wear a sword on ceremonial occasions?

Flags
47 In World War I, the sighting of a certain flag sometimes caused HM ships to hesitate before opening fire. What was the flag and why was this so?
48 Which letters of the International Code of Signals do the following patterns represent and what are their colours?

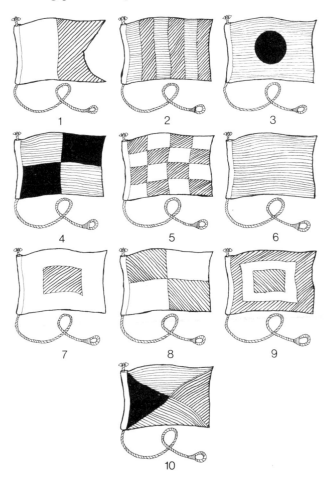

49 What flag does an Admiral of the Fleet fly?
50 In the International Code of Signals, what do the following flags signify?

(a) A		(f) O
(b) G		(g) V
(c) J		(h) W
(d) U		(i) Y
(e) D		(j) S

51 If at 'colours' in the morning an ensign has to be half-masted as a mark of respect for the death of a national figure, what is the rule on hoisting?
52 In a gaff rigged vessel, where is the ensign usually carried?
53 What is:
(a) a 'storm ensign'?
(b) a 'battle ensign'?
54 What is the slang name for a signalman in the Royal Navy?
55 When would a warship fly three Union flags at once?
56 Can you describe the flag which flies over the midship section of a warship being launched?
57 In what year was the white ensign made standard to the Royal Navy?
58 How did (a) British submarines and (b) German submarines indicate their successes on return from patrol?

Morse Code
59 What are the following letters in Morse code?

(a) E.		(f) Q.
(b) H.		(g) R.
(c) K.		(h) U.
(d) M.		(i) W.
(e) N.		(j) Y.

60 If a dot is taken as one unit in the Morse code, how many units make up a dash?
61 What does $\overline{AA}$ $\overline{AA}$ $\overline{AA}$ etc. mean?

Signals with a Smile
62 From corvette returning to base to motor torpedo boat setting out on patrol: 'Good Luck'. Reply from MTB: 'Thanks. Actually . . .'
Can you complete the MTB's reply?

63 From Admiralty to WRNS training establishment: 'Reference Admiralty letter dated . . . For sexy quality read. . .

Can you complete the signal?

64 When HMS *Queen Elizabeth* and the Cunard liner *Queen Elizabeth* met for the first time in the Atlantic, what was the single-word signal?

65 The destroyer, HMS *Diamond* had just collided with the cruiser HMS *Swiftsure* during manoeuvres at sea. Technically, the destroyer was in the wrong. When the two ships had extricated themselves, the *Swiftsure* sent this signal to the *Diamond*: 'What do you intend to do now?'

What was the destroyer captain's now famous reply?

66 Ships are assembled to show the Royal Navy's respect to HM the Queen in a time honoured way. Unfortunately, one commanding officer is a little shaky on his protocol and makes a signal to a neighbouring ship to find out the correct form.

First ship to second ship: 'Interrogative, 2 hips or 3?' Reply: '2, as in Marilyn Monroe!'

Why should ship no 1 be seeking such information?

67 From flagship to cruiser which is out of station: 'What are you doing?'

Can you provide the two-word reply?

The 'Andrew' Lingo

68 How did the Royal Navy come to be nick-named the 'Andrew'?

69 Who was responsible for the introduction into the navy of 'hard-lying money' and what is it?

70 What does the term 'all Harry Tate' mean and how did it come about?

Naval Nicknames

71 These nicknames are jumbled up. Can you correct the list, giving each surname the traditional nickname afforded it by sailors?

(a) 'Dodger'	Bird	(i) 'Pincher'	Murphy
(b) 'Knocker'	Clark	(j) 'Spud'	Palmer
(c) 'Dusty'	Dean	(k) 'Taff'	Young
(d) 'Hookey'	Evans	(l) 'Froggy'	Walker
(e) 'Pedlar'	French	(m)'Tug'	Tanner
(f) 'Dickie'	Long	(n) 'Bob'	White
(g) 'Nellie'	Martin	(o) 'Brigham'	Wilson
(h) 'Nobby'	Miller		

Food and Drink to a Sailor

72 Why, in the early days, was beer a staple drink aboard ship?
73 What was 'burgoo'?
74 What was the 'maggot Derby'?
75 What was sometimes known as 'schooner on the rocks'?
76 What were termed in the seamen's messes 'Port and Starboard oars'?
77 What are 'herrings in'?
78 When the seaman sits down to a portion of 'whales', what is he talking about?
79 Who is the 'spud barber'?

100 Nautical Terms and Expressions

Can you give the meaning of the following 100 terms?

1 Alee.
2 Airport.
3 Arming.
4 Avast.
5 Beam ends.
6 Belting.
7 'Between the devil and the deep blue sea'.
8 Bill of lading.
9 Bitter end.
10 Bogey.
11 Break sheer.
12 Bowse down.
13 Barrack stanchion.
14 Barge (in the Royal Navy).
15 'On the beach'.
16 'Belay the last pipe'.
17 A bluff.
18 Bullocks.
19 Buzz.
20 Capping.
21 Clew up.
22 Coaming.
23 Cod end.
24 Dan.
25 Dead marine.
26 Ditty box.

27 Dolly.
28 To drip.
29 Dghaisa.
30 'Flog the cat'.
31 Flying angel.
32 Flying jib.
33 Forefoot.
34 Foyboat.
35 Frostbiter.
36 Galley packet.
37 Gingerbread work.
38 Grabbies.
39 Grain (other than in a piece of timber).
40 Green rub.
41 Gobbie.
42 Grommet.
43 Guzz.
44 Harness cask.
45 Hoveller.
46 Irish pendants.
47 Jankers.
48 Jury.
49 'Ki'.
50 Killick.
51 Knightheads.
52 Levanter.
53 Last dog.
54 Log fender.
55 Loom.
56 Maltese lace.
57 Manifest.
58 Mess traps.
59 Mud hook.
60 Muzzler.
61 Nip.
62 One bell.
63 Palm.
64 Pier head jump.
65 Poodle faker.
66 The putty.
67 (a) Pusser.
(b) Pusser's dip.
(c) Pusser's dirk.
(d) Pusser's crabs.
(e) Pusser's medal.
(f) Pusser's hard.
68 Queen Bee.
69 'In the rattle'.
70 Rogue's salute.
71 Reef earings.
72 Saddle.
73 Scran.
74 To shiver.
75 Skate.
76 Slops.
77 Snob.
78 Snowball hitch.
79 To snub.
80 Spithead pheasant.
81 Sponson.
82 Stone frigate.
83 Sullage.
84 To swallow the anchor.
85 Swatchway.
86 Sweeper.
87 Sprog.
88 Squeegee band.
89 Steaming covers.
90 To swing the lead.
91 Taffrail.
92 Tiddie-oggie.
93 Triatic stay.
94 Trot.
95 Two blocks.
96 To 'warm the bell'.
97 'Wet as a scrubber'.
98 Wharfinger.
99 Whelps.
100 Yaw.

5
Submarines

General

1 How do submariners refer to their submarines?
2 What was the early nickname for the Submarine Service?
3 Who designed the first torpedo that could steer itself under its own power?
4 What is a stop trim?
5 What metal does the Soviet Union use for its very deep-diving submarines?
6 How quickly could a World War II U-boat dive?

The Beginnings

7 Who remarked of whom that he 'was the greatest fool that ever existed to encourage a mode of warfare which those who commanded the seas did not want and which, if successful, could deprive them of it'?
8 What was the first underwater craft to attempt an attack?
9 What was the first submarine to make a successful attack?
10 What was the connection between Britain's first practicable (but non-naval) submarine *Resurgam* of 1879 and London's underground railway trains of the time? Who was the inventor and what was his profession?
11 Which was the first warship to be sunk by a self-propelled torpedo?
12 Who designed HM Submarine No 1 (1901) and what was the original intention for his submarine inventions?

Submarine Successes

13 What did Churchill call the 'Beast' and who, in September

1943, made sure the 'Beast' would never leave its lair to prowl again?

14 What was the principal task of British and Allied submarines in the Mediterranean from July 1940 to May 1943?

15 What was the first vessel to pierce the North Pole and open up the long-sought North West Passage?

16 Why has it been said that the two atom bombs dropped on Hiroshima and Nagasaki in August 1945 were unnecessary?

17 In World War II which ship sank five enemy submarines, and shared in the sinking of a sixth, in the space of twelve days?

18 What was the largest warship to be sunk by a submarine?

Escape

19 Who made the first successful submarine escape?

20 What happened to K13?

21 What caused HMS *Thetis* to sink in Liverpool Bay in 1939?

22 Why was the use of oxygen discontinued for escape sets?

23 In August 1973, the world held its breath as two men entombed in a submersible 1,575ft down on the Atlantic seabed, waited for rescue. What was the name of their craft?

24 From how deep can submarine escapes now be made?

Not so Serious

25 If a submarine on the surface had its 'bird bath' rigged, what would the weather be like?

26 What in the early days was the submariner's equivalent of canaries down a mine?

27 Who created Leading Stoker Bootle, the oily and devious submariner of the BBC's and British Forces Broadcasting Service's series of radio stories?

28 How did submariners, until the 1960s, 'get their own back'?

29 What is 'train smash' on a menu?

30 Who is 'scratch'?

6

Sea Personalities

Nelson Himself

1 (a) At which battle did Nelson put his telescope to his blind eye saying 'I have a right to be blind sometimes. I really do not see the signal!'
  (b) What was the signal he was affecting not to see?
2 (a) Which was Nelson's favourite ship?
  (b) Where was she built?
3 What was Nelson's last signal at Trafalgar?
4 In Nelson's time, what was a 'tarpaulin captain'?
5 Where did Nelson lose his right arm?
6 How did Nelson lose the sight of his right eye?
7 What were star, bar and canister?
8 At Trafalgar, a British, French and Spanish ship each had the same name. What was the name?
9 Who was the First Lord of the Admiralty at the time of Trafalgar?
10 What finally happened to Nelson's 'bequest to the nation', Lady Hamilton?
11 If a sailor of Nelson's time used the word 'lobster', what would he have been talking about?
12 After what action did Nelson speak highly of the 69th Regiment of Foot (later the Welch [sic] Regiment).

Sailors through History

13 Who commanded the Enterprise of England, what was the Enterprise of England, and who was the original commander?
14 Who was the signal expert who went down with the HMS *Royal George* when she capsized at Spithead in 1782?

15 He was at the Battle of Bunker Hill in the American War of Independence in 1775, and was buried in the crypt of St Paul's alongside Nelson, in 1810. What was his name?

16 In February 1942, Vice-Admiral Otto Ciliax's name became famous in the British press. Why?

17 Who was the highest scoring U-boat captain in the history of the German navy?

18 Who was the highest scoring submarine captain in the history of the Royal Navy?

19 He joined Admiral Beatty's Flagship, HMS *Lion*, in 1916, but missed the Battle of Jutland by six weeks. In World War II he was almost sunk three times, and actually sunk once. He served in almost every type of ship, and was captain of the aircraft carrier HMS *Illustrious* for three months. He was still on the Active List when he died. Who was he?

20 The daughter of a New Zealand sheep farmer, she was newly married and with only a couple of years limited sailing experience behind her. In June 1978, she made sailing history although she had never handled a boat alone before.
   (a) What was her name?
   (b) What was her achievement?

21 He was royal, and is said on one particular occasion to have bumped his head on a deck beam when he stood up. (History has it that this is why the navy enjoys the unique privilege of drinking the Sovereign's health sitting down, though there are several theories.) While a serving naval officer in the West Indies he acted as best man at Captain Horatio Nelson's wedding to the charming widow, Mrs Nisbet.
   (a) What was his name?
   (b) What is the nickname often given him?

22 In 1497 he made an extensive voyage westward, reaching land and believing, like Columbus, that he had come to the coast of Asia. He had navigated via Iceland and the coast of Greenland eventually sailing some 2,000 miles down the seaboard of North America.
   (a) What was his name?
   (b) What was the name of his son who, history has it, took a great deal of the credit for his father's voyages?

23 He joined the navy as a seaman and swiftly rose to the rank of Master, his surveying of the St Lawrence River playing an

important part in the capture of Quebec in 1759. His later voyages made history. What was his name?

24 A brilliantly coloured flower was named after a French naval officer and explorer. What is the name of this flower?

25 He was known as 'Old Grog' because he wore a grogram coat. He was also famous for instituting the watering down of the sailor's daily ration of rum. What was his name?

26 As an admiral, he had fought with his fleet to relieve Minorca at the beginning of the Seven Years' War in 1756, but according to his accusers had not 'done his utmost to engage the enemy'. This was a capital offence under one of the Articles of War, and he therefore faced execution. What was his name and how did he meet his end?

27 He was the first navigator to sail completely round the world by steering to westward. What was his name?

28 The original leader of the expedition which set out in September 1519, is far more famous in history, and is 'credited' with having been the first to circumnavigate the globe. What was his name and what happened to him?

29 In 1576, he set out on the first of three voyages to the Arctic, with the object of discovering the North West Passage. What was his name?

30 When master of the brig *Rebecca* in 1731, he claimed he was boarded by a Spanish coastguard and that a part of his anatomy had been cut off. He later displayed this to Parliament in a jar of pickle. What was his name, what was his exhibit and what did his action lead to?

31 As Second Sea Lord he founded the training colleges for officers at Dartmouth and Osborne and had schools for seamen built in the dockyard towns. Later, as First Sea Lord, he was responsible for scrapping a large number of the Navy's ships. 'Scrap the lot' was his phrase. He also introduced a particular type of battleship. What was his name and what was the name of the first of his new battleships?

32 He charged a friend with treason and mutiny, convened a 'court of law', complete with jury, and condemned him to death. He then took Holy Communion with this same 'friend' before his execution. What was his name and what was the name of his friend?

33 He was a protégé of Churchill's and with his bulldog

expression, and his habit of wearing his cap rather on one side epitomised the British concept of the 'sea dog'. His commands included a gunboat on the River Nile, and a battleship on the China station. What was his name?

34 She was born at Surbiton, Surrey and began sailing at the age of five. Having received her secondary education at the Royal Ballet School, she studied economics and embarked on a career in marketing. However she abandoned the city life as the call of the sea proved irresistible. What is her name?

35 He has been sailing and cruising for well over half a century. A frequent winner of races in bad weather, in 1957 he was elected Yachtsman of the Year. He has written many books, some of which have almost become yachtsmen's 'bibles'. What is his name?

36 Born in Hawick, Scotland, he won a round-the-world race with a crew of soldiers. Taking just over 144 days, he equalled the record of the famous grain clippers. For a remarkable exploit in 1966, he was awarded the BEM. Later after another venture he termed 'the impossible voyage', he received the CBE. What is his name?

37 It has been said of him that he was one of the last genuine English eccentrics. Friend of princes and paupers alike, he was an outstanding designer. In 1928, his planing dinghy collected fifty-two wins in as many weeks. He was a choirboy 'which gave me an understanding of music that brought peace and quiet to my mind through many a dark hour ever since'. Who was he?

38 She founded the Royal Sailors' Rests at Devonport, Portsmouth and Chatham, and sailors gave her a nickname. What were her name and nickname?

39 He was born in Nova Scotia in 1844, ran away from home at the age of twelve and earned his living as a cabin boy among fishermen of the Bay of Fundy. He grew up to become a boatbuilder, naval architect, fisherman, shipowner and lone sailor. What was his name?

40 It was said of him that he was 'a navigator in the true Elizabethan sense'. He was certainly famous as a publisher of maps. Who was he?

41 He was born in Edinburgh in 1924; served with the merchant service from 1941, then after the war spent most of his sea-

faring career in the Far East. Home from Hong Kong, he bought a yacht and took his wife and family on an educational cruise around the world. Killer whales, however, brought the voyage to a sudden end in the Pacific, but he and his family survived. What are his name and the name of the boat?

42 He was founder of a sea school; and from 1938 was responsible for the training of yachtsmen for the RNVR and RAF Air Sea Rescue Service. He is a Master Mariner and a Fellow of both the Royal Institute of Navigation and the Royal Astronomical Society. It has been said of him that he is to the yachtsman what Hamleys is to the schoolboy. Certainly, in the maritime world, his business is as famous. What is his name?

7
Music Maritime

Opera and Ballet

1 What do these three operas have in common: *The Flying Dutchman (Der Fliegende Holländer)* by Wagner; *Otello* by Verdi; and *Peter Grimes* by Britten?

2 Who is Captain Balstrode?

3 'With . . . tread upon our prey we steal . . .'
With what kind of 'tread' upon their prey do whom steal?

4 This opera opens on an arid wild beach on the island of Ceylon (now called Sri Lanka) and contains a famous duet between two friends in love with the same girl.
(a) What is the opera?
(b) Who wrote it?
(c) Who are the two friends?

5 The 'Adagio of Spartacus and Phrygia' is now famous for a special reason.
(a) Why has it recently been brought to prominence?
(b) Where does it come from?
(c) Who composed it?

6 This opera was inspired by a holiday and is concerned with the wrecking and plunder of ships by the use of false navigation lights; and of the love of a Methodist minister's wife for a sailor with whom she works to prevent such terrorism.
(a) What is the name of the opera?
(b) Who wrote it?
(c) Where does the opera have its setting?

Music with a Salty Flavour

7 What connection do these two well-known works have with

48

the god of the sea: *Merrie England* by Edward German and *The Planets* by Gustav Holst?

8 *De l'aube à midi sur la mer* (*From dawn to midday on the sea*) is the first of three pieces inspired by the sea.
  (a) Who was the composer?
  (b) What is the title of the whole work?
  (c) Can you provide the titles of the other two pieces?

9 The following are movements from a choral work by an English composer: 'A Song for all Seas, all Ships'; 'On the Beach at Night Alone'; 'The Waves'; and 'The Explorers'.
  (a) Who was the composer?
  (b) What did he title the work?
  (c) Who wrote the words to which the music was set?

10 Which other composer used verse by the same poet as (c) above, naming the work after a set of poems called 'Sea Drift'?

11 Who used verses from Kipling's *Just So Stories* for his sea song 'Rolling Down to Rio'?

12 Who was the composer who is said to have confided to a friend 'I was intended for a fine career as a sailor'?

13 Who was the conductor whose arrangement of the traditional 'Sailor's Hornpipe' regularly gets such an enthusiastic reception at the Promenade Concerts?

14 (a) Who wrote music to these words?
   (b) What did he title the work?

> Sea birds are asleep,
> The world forgets to weep,
> Sea murmurs her soft slumber-song
> On the shadowy sand
> Of this elfin land . . .

Snatches of Shanties

15 Which sea shanties do these phrases come from?
  (a) . . . Weigh, hey and up she rises . . .
  (b) As I was a-walkin' down Paradise Street . . .
  (c) . . . 'cross the wide Missouri . . .
  (d) . . . singing fare ye well my bonny young lass . . .
  (e) . . . I took that maid upon my knee . . .
  (f) . . . I thought I heard the captain say . . .

8

The Royal Connection

In Music

1 What royal occasion brought together: A city company's barge; music from fifty instruments; and a progress 'all the way from Lambeth'?
2 Similarly, what royal occasion brought together: music by Elgar; Dame Clara Butt; and Balmoral Castle?
3 What famous song brings together: the First Lord; his family tree; and the monarch?

In History

4 What is the connection between: a Saxon sovereign; a south coast sea front; and Britain's volunteer navy?
5 (a) Who brought the Royal Marines into existence?
  (b) The Marines are afforded a unique privilege which dates from the same time. What is it?
6 (a) Who popularised the sailor's suit for small boys?
  (b) How did this come about?
7 For HM ships, the launching ceremony always used to be performed by a royal personage or a Royal Dockyard Commissioner.
  (a) Who had this rule relaxed?
  (b) How was the custom changed?
8 Legend has it that after his coronation, he rowed half a dozen inferior English kings in a boat on the River Dee, in Cheshire, while the newly crowned king helmed the boat with a steering oar. Who was the king in question?
9 In 1897, seven miles of ships assembled at Spithead to celebrate Queen Victoria's Diamond Jubilee.
  (a) Who took the salute on that occasion?

(b) What was his rank at the time?

10 Who is often termed 'the father of the English Navy'?

11 When dining formally in their messes, officers of the Royal Navy and Royal Marines drink the loyal toast while seated. But there is one exception to this custom. What is it?

9
I Name This Ship

1 How did the custom of breaking a bottle of wine over a ship's stem at her launching originate?

2 Why is the bottle at a launching ceremony always now secured to the ship by a lanyard?

3 After the Washington Conference in 1922, maritime nations agreed on their naval strength. As a result, Britain had to scrap a good many of her ships. But she was able within the Treaty limits to build two new battleships, both of which were given famous names. What were they?

4 A warship is always referred to by name with either 'HMS' or the definite article as a prefix. However, if a boat comes alongside and is hailed, the reply could be the name of the boat's parent ship without the use of a prefix, eg '*Vanguard*!' What does this reply mean?

5 Why does the Ships' Names Committee avoid, if possible, conferring long names on HM ships?

6 In 1857, this ship had to be launched sideways because of her great size and stuck several times on her way down the slip. What was the ship's name and who was her designer?

10
Who Wrote?

1 Who wrote the following?

The ideal dinghy crew would have these qualities:
  (i) Unquestioning obedience.
  (ii) Doesn't mind getting wet, cold and bored.
  (iii) Doesn't bruise easily.
  (iv) Doesn't complain when bruised.
  (v) Strong, silent and agile.
  (vi) Enjoys being blamed for things that aren't his fault.
  (vii) Has a bent towards telepathy.
  (viii) Impeccable timekeeper and recorder of courses.
  (ix) Naturally good eyesight for spotting distant buoys (desirable magnification on ordinary eyes, 4×30).
  (x) Likes winning.
  (xi) Very good when losing.
  (xii) Preferred hobbies: sewing, woodwork and swimming.

2 Who wrote these lines and what is the famous title that goes with them?

Come cheer up, my lads, 'tis to glory we steer,
To add something more to this wonderful year

3 Who wrote the following and of whom was he writing?

A fortnight later I saw . . . on board the *Rawalpindi*. I have never seen him so happy; he was like a child who has been given a new toy . . . His enthusiasm was unbounded, his pride immense. I knew then that the disappointments that had been rankling for the past eighteen years had vanished. They were forgotten in his passionate interest and pride in his new command.

4 Who wrote these lines?

> No one had ever been over the same terrible course twice with such an interval between. No one had felt its dangers and responsibilities from the summit as I had, or, to descend to a small point, understood how First Lords of the Admiralty are treated when great ships are sunk and things go wrong . . .
>
> And what of the supreme, measureless ordeal in which we were again irrevocably plunged? . . . We still had command of the sea. We were woefully outmatched in numbers in this new mortal weapon of the air. Somehow the light faded out of the landscape.

5 Who wrote the following and who is speaking?

> The ship was rolling scuppers under in the ocean swell. The booms were tearing at the blocks, the rudder was banging to and fro, and the whole ship was creaking, groaning and jumping like a manufactory. I had to cling to the backstay, and the world turned giddily before my eyes; for though I was a good enough sailor when there was way on, this standing still and being rolled about like a bottle was a thing I never learned to stand without a qualm or so, above all in the morning, on an empty stomach.

6 Who wrote this passage and in what book?

> *Moshulu* was running ten knots in the biggest seas I had ever seen. As I watched, the poop began to sink before my eyes, and the horizon astern was blotted out by a high polished wall, solid and impenetrable, like marble. The poop went on dropping until the whole ship seemed to be toppling backwards into the deep moat below the wall of water that loomed over her, down and down to the bottom of the sea itself. At the moment when it seemed that this impregnable mass must engulf us, a rift appeared in its face and it collapsed, burrowing beneath the ship, bearing her up so that what a moment before seemed a sluggish, solid hulk destined for the sea bed was now like a bird skimming the water, supported by the wind high above the valley.

7 The following passage is taken from a classic on sailing by a man who with his wife has sailed twice round the world in their 30ft sloop. Who is the writer and what was the name of their boat?

There are many different forms of the sport. One man gets his pleasure by making short day sails along the coast, spending each night at anchor, sharing with his wife and family the peace of the creeks and the novelty of life in their compact and mobile floating home. Another, who can spare the time, gets his satisfaction by making long passages in the open sea, taking the weather as it comes, and driving his yacht day and night until he fetches up in some foreign land. The cruising done by the majority, whose numbers are swelling steadily year by year, probably lies between these two extremes.

8 The following passage is taken from a book on power yachts by a well known designer and his wife. Who are they?

We have always held strong views on power yachts. They have often tended to be considered to be second-class citizens compared with sailing boats, and while this may have been true in the last century, it is certainly not so now. Sailing boats are lovely in themselves and only the most dismal versions are regarded as failures, but a power yacht is now often as complex as an aircraft and can be a disappointment if she is less than first class in every department. We wanted to try to put the principles of excellence in power yachts into our book, rather than to give a list of useful data or pages of design drawings which inevitably get out of date in a few years in this fast developing area of naval architecture.

9 This passage is taken from a classic sea adventure which was made into a film. Who wrote the book and what is its title?

'Can't I be of any use?'

'Oh, don't you bother', he answered. 'I expect you're tired. Aren't we having a splendid sail? That must be Ekken on the port bow,' peering under the sail, 'where the trees run in. I say, do you mind looking at the chart?' He tossed it over to me. I spread it out painfully, for it curled up like a watch-spring at the least slackening of pressure. I was not familiar with charts, and this sudden trust reposed in me after a good deal of neglect made me nervous.

'You see Flensburg, don't you?' he said. 'That's where we are', dabbing with a long reach at an indefinite space on the crowded sheet. 'Now, which side of that buoy off the point do we pass?'

10 Can you give the name of the Surveyor-General of Victualling who wrote this?

> Englishmen, and more especially seamen, love their bellies above everything else, and therefore it must always be remembered in the management of the victualling of the Navy, that to make any abatement from them in the quantity or agreeableness of the Victuals is to discourage and provoke them in their tenderest point, and will sooner render them disgusted with the King's service than any other hardship that can be put upon them.

11 Who was the writer of the following? Which book is it taken from, and what was the name of the ship which is the subject of the passage?

> The ship went forward at an easy ten knots, with the flood tide adding a couple more; the winter sunset, a lovely red and orange, made the bracken on the surrounding hillsides glow like fire. Moving through the still evening, parting the cold keen air with a steady thrust, the ship seemed to have a living purpose of her own, a quality of strength and competence: and Ericson found it hard to exclude from his voice, as he gave the helm orders that would lay a course through the defence-boom, the eagerness that possessed him. For . . . was clear: her engines and her armament were all in order: in a few days they would go north for their final working up, and then she would be ready . . .

12 Who wrote this of England?

> She has always owed her fortunes to the sea, and to the havens and rivers that from earliest times opened her inland regions to what the sea might bring. Long before she aspired to rule the waves she was herself their subject, for her destiny was continually being decided by the boat-crews which they floated to her shore.

II

Who Said?

Can you give the name of the speaker for each of the following quotations?

1 'There were gentlemen and there were seamen in the navy of Charles II. But the seamen were not gentlemen; and the gentlemen were not seamen.'

2 'Sink me the ship, Master Gunner! Sink her, split her in twain!'

3 'More dangerous than a battle once a week!' (describing the coast along the north-east corner of the Bay of Biscay, near Brest).

4 'Believe me, my young friend, there is *nothing*, absolutely nothing, half so much worth doing as simply messing about in boats.'

5 'On land I am a hero; at sea I am a coward!'

6 'Praise the Lord and pass the ammunition!'

7 'A man-of-war is the best ambassador.'

8 'I don't care if he drinks, gambles and womanises; he hits the target!'

9 'No man will be a sailor who has the contrivance to get himself in jail, for being in a ship is being in jail with a chance of being drowned. A man in jail has more room, better food and commonly better company!'

10 'The navy's here!'

11 'I have not yet begun to fight!'

12 'Wherever wood can swim, there I am sure to find this flag of England.'

12

Some Classical Clippings

1 (a) Who wrote these lines?
  (b) What is the full title of the poem they come from?
  (c) A heavenly body inspired the same poet to write another
      poem which has navigational connotations. Can you
      name the poem?

> The very deep did rot; O Christ!
> That ever this should be!
> Yea, slimy things did crawl with legs
> Upon the slimy sea. . . .

2 What is the title of this famous poem by Matthew Arnold and
  how does it end?

> The sea is calm tonight.
> The tide is full, the moon lies fair
> Upon the Straits; – on the French coast, the light
> Gleams, and is gone; the cliffs of England stand,
> Glimmering and vast, out in the tranquil bay.
> Come to the window, sweet is the night air!
>
> Only, from the long line of spray
> Where the ebb meets the moon-blanch'd sand,
> Listen! you hear the grating roar
> Of pebbles which the waves suck back, and fling,
> At their return, up the high strand . . .

3 The following lines are taken from the poem of a Poet
  Laureate writing about a county with a particularly beautiful
  coastline.

See . . . a pathetic sight,
Raddled and put upon and tired
And looking somewhat over-hired,
Remembering in the autumn air
The years when she was young and fair . . .

(a) Can you name the poet?
(b) What title did he give his poem?

4 (a) What poem do these lines come from?
(b) Who wrote them?

A treacherous monster is the Shark,
He never makes the least remark.
And when he sees you on the sand
He doesn't seem to want to land . . .

5 Who wrote the following lines?

The tide rises, the tide falls,
The twilight darkens, the curlew calls;
Along the sea-sands damp and brown
The traveller hastens toward the town;
And the tide rises, the tide falls.

6 Who wrote these lines and which poem do they come from?

He rose at dawn and, fired with hope,
  Shot o'er the seething harbour-bar,
And reach'd the ship and caught the rope,
  And whistled to the morning star.

And while he whistled long and loud
  He heard a fierce mermaiden cry,
'O boy, though thou art young and proud,
  I see the place where thou wilt lie.

'The sands and yeasty surges mix
  In caves about the dreary bay,
And on thy ribs the limpet sticks,
  And in thy heart the crawl shall play . . .'

7 Who wrote the words and music of the famous song:

> Oh! I do like to be beside the seaside,
> I do like to be beside the sea . . .

and can you complete the chorus?

8 In these lines by Sir Humphrey Davy what is meant by the Bolerium?

> On the sea
> The sunbeams tremble, and the purple light
> Illumines the dark Bolerium, seat of storms.

9 These lines are from a one-act musical play.

> Has anybody seen our Ship, the HMS Peculiar?
> We've been on shore for a month or more
> And when we see the captain we shall get what for . . .

(a) What is the name of the play?
(b) Who wrote it?

10 These are famous lines. Which poem do they come from and who wrote it?

> Call him on the deep sea, call him up the Sound,
> Call him when ye sail to meet the foe;
> Where the old trade's plyin' an' the old flag flyin'
> They shall find him ware and wakin', as they found him long
> ago!

11 The following lines are from the poem, 'Great Black-Backed Gulls', by John Heath-Stubbs:

> Said Cap'n . . . to Cap'n . . .
> Remember the grand times, Cap'n, when
> The . . . flapped on the tropic breeze,
> And we were terrors of the . . .

(a) Who were the two captains?
(b) Can you fill in the other missing words?
(c) What were the two captains noted for?

12 Who wrote the following (this is the first verse), and can you quote the opening line of the poem, thereby providing its title?

> . . . .
> That guard our native seas;
> Whose flag has braved, a thousand years,
> The battle and the breeze!
> Your glorious standard launch again
> To match another foe!
> And sweep through the deep,
> While the stormy tempests blow;
> While the battle rages loud and long,
> And the stormy tempests blow . . .

13 Who wrote these lines?

> Dream after dream I see the wrecks that lie
> Unknown of man, unmarked upon the charts,
> Known of the flat-fish with the withered eye,
> And seen by women in their aching hearts . . .

14 Who wrote the words to that most patriotic of songs: 'Rule Britannia'?

15 In which of Shakespeare's works are these lines to be found?

> Suppose that you have seen
> The well-appointed king at Hampton pier
> Embark his royalty; and his brave fleet
> With silken streamers the young Phoebus fanning:
> Play with your fancies, and in them behold
> Upon the hempen tackle ship-boys climbing;
> Hear the shrill whistle which doth order give
> To sounds confus'd . . .

16 These lines are by William Cowper:

> Toll for the brave –
> The brave that are no more!
> All sunk beneath the wave
> Fast by their native shore!

61

Eight hundred of the brave,
Whose courage was well tried,
Had made the vessel heel
And laid her on her side.

A land breeze shook the shrouds
And she was overset;
Down went the . . .
With all her crew complete.

Toll for the brave!
Brave . . . is gone;
His last sea fight is fought,
His work of glory done . . .

(a) What ship was the subject of the poem?
(b) Who had fought 'his last sea fight'?

17 The following is the first verse of a poem called 'The Ship to Rio'. Who wrote it?

There was a ship of Rio
Sailed out into the blue,
And nine and ninety monkeys
Were all her jovial crew.

18 Who speaks the following words and where are they to be found?

The sky, it seems, would pour down stinking pitch,
But that the sea, mounting to th' welkin's cheek,
Dashes the fire out. O! I have suffer'd
With those that I saw suffer: a brave vessel,
Who had, no doubt, some noble creatures in her,
Dash'd all to pieces.

19 (a) Can you complete the last lines of Masefield's famous poem?
   (b) What is its title?

Dirty British coaster with salt-caked smoke stack,
Butting through the Channel in the mad March days,
With a cargo of Tyne coal . . .

20 This brief observation is called 'Little Fish'. Who wrote it?

> The tiny fish enjoy themselves
> in the sea
> Quick little splinters of life,
> Their little lives are fun to them
> in the sea.

13
Sea Mysteries

1 She was a brigantine of 282 tons which had sailed out of New York harbour in November 1872. Bound for Genoa, her cargo was 1,700 barrels of alcohol for fortifying wines. The master had his wife and small daughter with him, together with seven crew.

   A month later, on a fine afternoon, she was discovered still sailing, but quite deserted, with her boat gone.
   (a) Who was she?
   (b) What was the name of the ship which found her?

2 On 29 April 1956 the Admiralty issued this brief official announcement:

   > He is presumed dead as a result of trials with certain underwater apparatus. The location was Stokes Bay, and it is nine days since the accident.

   (a) To whom was the announcement referring?
   (b) What were the circumstances of the said 'accident'?

3 The three masted merchant vessel *Marlborough* of Glasgow, sailed from Lyttelton in the South Island of New Zealand in January 1890 bound for England with a cargo of sheep.

   She was sighted off the Straits of Magellan on schedule, but after that was never seen or heard of again. That is, not for twenty-three years!
   (a) How and where was she found?
   (b) What was the state of the *Marlborough* and her crew when discovered?

4 A young man aboard the *Baccante* sailing between Melbourne and Sydney in 1881 recorded this account in the ship's log:

> The . . . crossed our bows. A strange red light, as of a phantom ship all aglow, in the midst of which light the masts, spars and sails of a brig two hundred yards distant stood up in strong relief. On arriving there, no vestige nor any sign whatever of any material ship was to be seen either near or right away to the horizon, the night being clear and the sea calm. Thirteen persons altogether saw her

(a) Who was the young man who made that entry in the log?
(b) What ship was he describing?

5 On 19 May 1845, the greatest polar expedition up to that time left England. This expedition was to make use of two steamships, each carrying a full complement of officers and men and with enough stores and provisions for three years.

But the two ships and their crews were to vanish, though years later some clues as to their fate gradually came to light from various search parties.

(a) Who was the explorer who led the expedition?
(b) What was the purpose of the expedition?

6 The legend of this lost continent was first recorded by the Greek philosopher, Plato, born about the year 428 BC. He told of a great land 'a country larger than Asia Minor with Libya situated just beyond the pillars of Hercules'. If it existed at all, modern geography places it opposite the present Strait of Gibraltar.

What continent was Plato referring to?

14

Creatures at Sea

Half a Name

1 Can you add the name of an animal, mammal or bird to the
following words to turn them into nautical terminology?

(a) . . . walk.
(b) . . . hitch.
(c) . . . nest.
(d) . . . house.
(e) . . . watch.
(f) . . . striker.
(g) . . . breakfast.
(h) . . . neck.

(i) . . . Latitudes.
(j) . . . island.
(k) . . . iron.
(l) . . . lines.
(m). . . horn.
(n) . . . star.
(o) . . . fist.

Birds of the Feathered Variety

2 Off what sort of coast would you expect to see:
(a) razorbills?
(b) guillemots?
(c) purple sandpipers?
3 Which is the only wader you may find happily *swimming* at
sea?
4 If you saw common terns ahead of you in the English
Channel, what would be the time of year?
5 What do you understand by the word 'rafting'?
6 What *land* bird is most likely to make a nest on your boat at
moorings?
7 What is the only seabird with no hind toe?
8 What is the difference between a ruff and a reeve?
9 How would you discriminate between a cormorant and a
shag?

10 What birds are associated with the following collective nouns?

(a) A wisp. (e) A spring.
(b) A trip. (f) A herd.
(c) A skein. (g) A flight.
(d) A gaggle.

11 A male swan is called a cob. What is the female called?

12 Describe a 'seaslater'?

13 What do you understand by 'Mother Carey's Chickens'?

15
Quiz from All Quarters

1 What is the equivalent army rank to a naval captain?
2 What are the 'chops of the Channel'?
3 What was a Viking's funeral?
4 The old hobby of decorating shells, whale's teeth etc, has a particular term to describe it. What is it?
5 What is the perigee of the moon?
6 On what date did sailors in the navy receive their last issue of a tot of rum?
7 What is drudging?
8 The world's largest ocean is the Pacific. What is its area (in square miles)?
9 What is 'spermaceti'?
10 A sailing vessel head to wind after raising anchor, or failing to go about, is in what condition?
11 What is the term to describe the drift astern that is the result of the above condition?
12 Who was the first European credited with the sighting of the Pacific Ocean?
13 The sinking of the county class cruiser HMS *Hampshire* off the north-east coast of Scotland in 1916 had a particular significance. What was it?
14 Which was the ship associated with Darwin?
15 Who engineered the Suez Canal?
16 What is the traditional wording for a ship's captain in a Lloyds insurance policy?
17 How does a sailor surge a rope?
18 What is meant by the term to 'wear ship'?
19 What is St Elmo's Fire?
20 What and where are the Roaring Forties?
21 What was a powder monkey?
22 What were hammock nettings in the days of sailing warships?

23 Which was the Royal Navy's first guided missile ship?
24 Where is Post Office Bay?
25 Where is the greatest archipelago in the world?
26 The Sail Training Association operates two almost identical topsail schooners, the *Sir Winston Churchill* and the *Malcolm Miller*. How may they be distinguished at a glance?
27 Why is Murmansk important?
28 Where is the Golden Horn?
29 What is the Humbolt Current?
30 What is an 'octant'?
31 What is the difference between shrouds and stays?
32 What is a 'red duster'?
33 What is the difference between a flashing and an occulting light?
34 If a fisherman hung a pair of oilskin trousers upside down in the rigging what would he be trying to tell you?
35 What is the signal for SOS in morse code?
36 What does the following describe? 'A set of stays leading outwards from the mainmast and upwards to a platform above to take the strain off the topmast stays.'
37 How would you describe in a word the act of emptying a sail of wind by easing sheets?
38 What is the 'trenail method'?
39 What is the parrot perch?
40 What is the 'yellow peril'?
41 What is meant by the 'deep V design'?
42 In marine terms, what are Rolls-Royce, Perkins, Kelvin, Gardner, Leyland and Ford all famous for?
43 What is the purpose of a reduction gear?
44 What is meant by indirect injection?
45 What do the following stand for?
   (a) CCA.
   (b) OSC.
   (c) RINA.
   (d) RNSA.
46 What is a Great Circle route?
47 Narwhal, right, and blue are all types of what?
48 Which is the brightest star in the heavens?
49 Who designed the delightful little 20ft cruiser, the *Westcoaster* – the forerunner of all the Westerly boats?

50 What is meant by 'three parts shot away'?

51 When, and to what ship, did the *Queen Mary* lose the 'Blue Riband' (the notional trophy for the fastest sea crossing of the Atlantic)?

52 What was *English Rose III*

53 What was the Board of Longitude?

54 What is a 'bare boat' charter?

55 What is a bumboat?

56 What was a 'Camship'?

57 Which is the most westerly cape of northern Spain?

58 Who was the discoverer of the St Lawrence River, in Canada?

59 What is the name of the iron band on the end of a bowsprit and fitted with eyes to take the bowsprit shrouds and the bobstay?

60 What is a mudhook?

61 What was the Chatham Chest?

62 What is a 'chubasco'?

63 Why was Iwo Jima important during World War II?

64 What is a drumhead?

65 Who was the first European to discover the sea route to India?

66 She was launched at Erith, Kent, in June 1514 and at some 1,000 tons was in her day the largest warship in the world. She was built by the master shipwright, William Bond, at the command of Henry VIII and was armed with twenty-one heavy (bronze) guns. What was her name?

67 Who constructed *Ra* and *Ra II* and what for?

68 Which capital ship was named after the Duke of Wellington and launched by the Duchess in 1912?

69 What are *Hoshi* and *Provident*, and what is the connection between them?

70 With whom do you associate the name *Pen Duick*?

71 What were the 'Strength Through Joy' ships?

72 How may the name of a well-known chairman of British Rail be connected with Nelson?

73 What is the longitude of the prime meridian?

74 What is a 'tarpaulin muster'?

75 What was significant about the *Yamato* and the *Musashi*?

Answers

1 A QUESTION OF SEAMANSHIP

Sailing

1 (a) Forward of the beam.
  (b) On the beam.
  (c) Abaft the beam.
2 The jib is backed and the tiller pushed down to leeward.
3 When sailing to windward it is frequently advantageous to take the tide on the lee bow as it can help to push the yacht towards the required track. It is of particular significance when racing.
4 When she is under sail and making headway though there is almost no wind.
5 One hand for yourself, one for the ship.
6 Illustration 1.
7 When 'swigging' or 'sweating-up' the halyards, eg by making a turn on the cleat, then taking up the slack on the halyard by hauling horizontally on its standing part.
8 The 'Cunningham' is a hole placed in the luff of a mainsail a few inches above the tack, and used to adjust the draught in the sail. Cunningham holes are also found in the mainsail leech and genoa luff.
9 The windward side.
10 Close hauled on the starboard tack.
11 The lubber line.
12 Name the points of the compass in order going round full circle.
13 The spoke of a steering wheel which is uppermost (and usually has on it some identifying mark) when the wheel is amidships.
14 A drying rock. (Its drying elevation above chart datum may also be given alongside in brackets.)
15 You are probably witnessing the approach of a 'line squall' which will hit you very suddenly and likely with great force.

Shorten sail as quickly as possible; prepare for a sudden shift of wind and tend tiller, sheets and halyards.

16 You are approaching a vessel moving across from right to left, but which is restricted in her ability to manoeuvre. Keep well clear; keep a careful watch on her, and be prepared to take further avoiding action.

17 It is the starboard sidelight of a sailing vessel which could be running on either side so as to involve the risk of collision. Assume you are the give-way vessel and go about to show your own green sidelight.

18 A small compass fixed to the deckhead in the captain's cabin which enables him to watch the helmsman's course while lying in his bunk!

19 Spars and rigging kept aloft; also any deckhouses, deck cargo, etc, that present windage.

20 'Set' is the direction towards which the tide flows. 'Drift' is the distance over which the current has acted, ie rate × time.

21 She is sailing her best close to the wind, ie 'close hauled'.

22 'Perfect safety, go ahead.' (The joke version is: 'Red to red, green to green, Perfect safety – go between'. This would, of course, result in disaster!)

23 A yacht under 7m in length. A sternlight. An anchor light. An open boat under oars. The masthead light of a vessel hull-down. A shore light. Venus rising! (Or as is often told to young trainees by seasoned instructors: 'the coxswain lighting another cigarette!')

24 (a) Flood tide stream of 5 knots in the direction of the arrow.

(b) One knot of *current* in the direction of the arrow.

25 By day, a cone, pointing downwards and hoisted forward where it can best be seen.

26 When the rudder is shaped and supported in such a way that a proportion of its underwater area (though not more than a third) lies forward of the axis of rotation.

27 It can give an indication of abnormal height of the tide. High pressure will tend to bring about a lower level of water at high tide, and vice versa.

28 Yes. He should have an anchor prepared and ready to let go, in case he needs it in a hurry.

29 Reading from the top band of the arch, the colours of the

rainbow are: red, orange, yellow, green, blue, indigo and violet. (We are considering the primary rainbow, of course. Should you also see above it the secondary rainbow, you may notice that the colours are ranged in the opposite order.)

30 Put the tiller to starboard. As she gathers sternway, the boat will then build up steerage way which, with backed jib, will help to cast the bow away to starboard. The boom might also be pushed across to windward.

Sails and Sailmaking

Sails

31 A spitfire jib, or storm jib.

32 A Spanish reef.

33 A headsail used when running. Safer than a spinnaker as it does not have to be re-set when gybing the mainsail.

34 A triangular sail set above a square sail, eg in a topsail schooner.

35 When the wind is free, studding sails can be set at the side of principal square sails to catch more wind and increase the ship's speed.

36 A narrow strip of sail set abaft the leech of a boom and gaff sail.

37 Additional canvas laced to the foot of a sail to increase its area and therefore catch more wind in fine weather.

38 A 'dandy'.

39 Lower it or furl it in a hurry!

40 Trice up the tack and drop the head of a peak to reduce sail area quickly. Mostly applied to gaff rigged vessels.

Sailmaking

41 Port side.

42 The patches incorporated into the tack, head and clew of a sail for extra strength.

43 A form of cross-stitching which is used when repairing sails in order to hold the seams flat.

44 (a) The arched curve in the foot of a square sail which enables the sail to clear fore and aft mast stays.

(b) The curved leech (the trailing edge) of a fore-and-aft sail.

Rig
45 Lugsail. The type of rig in this case is usually known as 'a standing lug'.
46 (a) Throat halyard
   (b) Gaff jaws
   (c) Mast hoops
   (d) Tack
   (e) Reef pendants
   (f) Reef points
   (g) Topping lift
   (h) Gaff mainsail
   (i) Gaff
   (j) Peak halyard
47 1 Gaff yawl
   2 Bermudian cutter
   3 Wishbone ketch
   4 Staysail schooner
   5 Gaff sloop
   6 Cat (or Scow)
48 *Jibs*
   1 Flying jib
   2 Outer jib
   3 Inner jib
   4 Jib or fore topmast staysail

Staysails
   1 Main topmast staysail
   2 Main topgallant staysail
   3 Royal staysail
   4 Mizzen topmast staysail
   5 Mizzen topgallant staysail

Foremast A
   1 Foresail (or course)
   2 Lower fore topsail
   3 Upper fore topsail
   4 Lower foretopgallant sail
   5 Upper foretopgallant sail
   6 Fore royal

Mainmast B
1 Mainsail (or course)
2 Lower main topsail
3 Upper main topsail
4 Lower main topgallant sail
5 Upper main topgallant sail
6 Main royal
7 Main skysail

Mizzenmast C
1 Crossjack (furled)
2 Lower mizzen topsail
3 Upper mizzen topsail
4 Mizzen topgallant sail
5 Mizzen royal
6 Spanker or driver

What Is and What Are?

Gear
49 Specifically, a round block, with three holes in it through which shroud lanyards are rove. Used to taughten shrouds and so named because they are not fitted with a sheave. But nowadays, virtually any eye with no sheave.
50 A conical wooden pin used for easing apart the strands of a rope when splicing it. Also wooden or steel support block for a top mast.
51 A double block with one sheave above the other rather than side by side.
52 A small tackle containing a single and double block fitted with a rope and used variously to increase purchase when hauling.
53 A long, heavy oar.
54 A block purchase used to haul down the tack of a sail.
55 A pole with jaws at one end and a spike at the other used to hold the jib out from the mast when the yacht is 'goosewinging'.
56 An oblong of oakum or matting laid virtually anywhere to prevent chafe.
57 Crutches.

58 Hollows cut in the gunwale of a boat into which the oars are slotted when rowing.

Parts of Ship
59 The sliding wooden hatch which leads to the cabin of a small boat.
60 A small spar holding out the bobstay below the bowsprit to give better downward pull on the bowsprit.
61 Iron rails carrying belaying pins which are fitted around the base of a mast. Also, the rails erected on the bulwarks which bounded the poop and quarterdeck of the old sailing men-o-war.
62 A gammon iron.
63 A jib-boom is a spar or boom which serves as an extension to the bowsprit to enable the carrying of a flying jib.
64 A board lowered on the lee side of a flat bottomed vessel to prevent drift to leeward.
65 Simply another name for the dolphin striker.
66 Parrel.
67 The strake beneath the gunwale on the topside.
68 Thole pins. In some craft the oar is slotted over a single pin and thus swivels on it.

Construction
69 Dodgers.
70 That part of her stern upon which the name is written.
71 The garboard strakes.
72 The fore and aft centreline plank on a wooden decked vessel.
73 Lapstrake.
74 A room with a large floor space on which boat plans are drawn up full size.
75 An instrument used when caulking to open up the seams to take the oakum.
76 A 'stealer'.
77 The fashion pieces – the aftermost timbers forming the shape of the stern.
78 1 Round bilge.
   2 Single chine.
   3 Double chine.

Anchoring

79 1 Danforth. 2 CQR. 3 Grapnel.
80 Fisherman's anchor.

1 Ring.	8 Crown (or Base).
2 Pin.	9 Shank (or Beam).
3 Folding stock.	10 Fluke.
4 Ball.	11 Balancing band.
5 Bill (or Pea).	12 Shoulder piece.
6 Palm.	13 Head.
7 Arm.	

81 1 Checking the vicinity of each craft and allowing enough room for swing.

2 Not letting go your own cable such that it will cross another boat's. Also, on a big ship, making sure there isn't a small boat under the bow.

3 Checking the nature of the bottom.

4 Paying out enough cable.

5 Ensuring you are clear of the channel or other restricted areas.

6 Hoisting the anchor ball or showing the anchor light or lights.

7 Allowing for the tidal rise and fall at the point of anchoring.

8 Checking the likely current.

9 Taking account of the weather in the coming period, and

10 Its effects on your shelter.

Other considerations are:

Don't let the cable pile up on the bottom.

Depending on size, correct amount of sternway on the vessel to pay out the cable along the bottom.

State of readiness of engines.

Depth. The anchor may be let go in shallow water, but may have to be 'walked' out on the windlass in any deep water.

Fixing or monitoring the vessel's position.

82 (a) Bower anchors.
    (b) In a hawsepipe, each side of the bow.
    (c) The 'sheet' or kedge anchor.
83 (a) A piece of flat metal placed to prevent damage to the ship's planking from chafe by mooring lines or cables.
    (b) The pipe down which the cable is led to the cable locker.
    (c) A small drum attached to a winch. Sometimes applied to the sprocket wheel of a windlass shaped to take the cable links as they pass round.
    (d) A light line attached to the crown of an anchor by which the anchor can be capsized or 'tripped' if necessary to clear any obstruction on the bottom. The line is usually buoyed.
84 Aboard a yacht, the kedge is a smaller anchor which is more easily handled than the main anchors in an emergency. For instance, it can be rowed out in a dinghy to haul off the yacht if it has gone aground. In racing, a kedge is also used when becalmed to hold the vessel against the tide.
85 'Anchor's a-weigh!'

Three in One

86 Dolphin.
87 Gripe.
88 Luff.
89 Tack.
90 Rum.
91 Sole.

Knotty Problems

Knots and Not Knots
92 1 Round turn and two half hitches.
    2 Clove hitch.
    3 Double sheet bend.
    4 Rolling hitch.
    5 Single carrick bend.
    6 Timber hitch and half hitch.
    7 Sheepshank.
    8 Fisherman's bend.
    9 Figure-of-eight.
  10 Overhand knot.

11 Bowline.
12 Surgeon's knot.
13 Catspaw.
14 Marling hitch.
15 Spanish bowline.
16 Bowline on the bight.
17 Jury knot.
18 Cow hitch.
19 Heaving-line bend.
20 Monkey's fist.

93 1 Securing a dinghy painter to a mooring ring.
    2 Securing temporarily to a bollard; burgee halyard to burgee stick; holding tiller control when boat at anchor.
    3 Joining two lines together. Securing the sheet to the clew of a sail. Double sheet bend is more secure and less likely to jamb than a single sheet bend.
    4 Used for making fast a line to a round spar or another rope, usually of larger diameter, when the load on one is to be parallel or nearly so to that of the other, eg taking the strain off an anchor cable with a warp.
    5 Used for joining two warps together when the join will have to pass round the barrel of a windlass or winch.
    6 Securing a rope to a log or spar to be lifted or towed.
    7 Used to shorten temporarily a length of rope.
    8 Bending a warp to an anchor.
    9 A stopper knot used to prevent the end of a line passing through an eye or block.
    10 Used as temporary stopper knot to prevent fraying, or to stop a line passing through an eye or sheave. But it can jamb particularly when wet, and a figure-of-eight is more seamanlike.
    11 Used to form a standing loop in the end of a line.
    12 Very similar to the reef knot, but more secure; specially when using synthetic ropes which tend to be slippery.
    13 Ideal for hitching a sling to a hook.
    14 Lashing a furled sail to its boom, or along the guardrail. Also used for lashing up a hammock.
    15 Can be used for a bosun's chair, or securing a ladder over the side, as staging for the painting party!

16 Makes a very serviceable bosun's chair when one is needed in a hurry. Two loops give more support.

17 The unfortunate dismasted sailor would find this one useful at the top of the jury mast he would have to rig. The knot forms the band at the top of a jury mast to which shrouds and stays are secured.

18 To secure a line to a spar or ring when load will come onto both ends of the line on the same side of the ring or spar. It won't jamb and is therefore easily released.

19 Self explanatory. Used for bending a heaving line onto the bight or eye of a mooring warp.

20 The traditional knot that gives weight to the end of a heaving line.

94 A 'bend' is used for joining two ropes together or securing a rope to an eye, ring or becket which may be easily cast off. In a 'hitch' the loops jamb together, specially under strain, but should be easily separable when the strain is taken off. No, they are not 'knots'. A knot is (usually) decorative, eg a Turk's Head.

95 Work it in the hand and tap it with a piece of wood or similar implement, or even roll it underfoot on the deck. The use of a marlin spike may damage the fibres.

96 It has been 'moused'.

Rope

97 (a) Grassline or coir rope.
   (b) It is less strong than other rope and is unsuitable for working with blocks and tackles.
   (c) It is light in weight, is springy and floats.

98 Hard fibres taken from Aloe (botanical name *Agave sisalana*) leaves. Almost white in colour and very strong. Indigenous to Bahamas and Yucatan, but also cultivated in East Africa and other countries.

99 (a) A method of coiling a rope by flaking it to and fro in parallel bends so that it may run out freely.
   (b) A rope so coiled on the deck is said to be 'cheesed'. This can also be termed a 'Flemish coil'.
   (c) When it will be required to run through a block, because the rope will inevitably form kinks as it is run off from the coil.

100 They are the various stages of covering a length of rope with canvas and yarn to protect the rope from chafe.

101 The loose end to be hauled upon.

102 A line rove through a block aloft and used for hoisting anything, ie a bosun's chair.

103 Small line consisting of two twisted strands. Usually used for binding round ropes and cables to prevent chafing.

104 The loose fibres of old hemp rope that has been picked to pieces. Used for caulking seams, stopping leaks, etc.

A Sailor's Forecasting

General

105 (a) 1854.

(b) The Board of Trade.

106 They both record pressure. A barograph also produces a continuous record on a chart.

107 Lines joining places of equal barometric pressure.

108 At sea, winds are deflected about 15° towards the low pressure.

109 Fog!

110 A tropical cyclone off Australasia (the Australians' name for a hurricane).

111 (a) Within 6 hours.

(b) 6–12 hours.

(c) In more than 12 hours.

112 10m (or approximately 33ft).

113 1 Showers.   4 Rain.

2 Thunderstorm.   5 Snow.

3 Fog.   6 Drizzle.

114 Yes, but the actual pressure is irrelevant. If looking towards the centre of the system pressure is increasing then it is a High. If looking towards the centre of the system pressure is decreasing, it is a Low.

The High of 1016 would more often than not feature fair weather with winds blowing clockwise around it; whereas the Low would probably feature unsettled weather with winds blowing anticlockwise around it.

Come Wind and Weather

115 Stand with your back to the wind, low pressure then lies to your left (in the Northern Hemisphere). Buys Ballot's law.

116 The wind as indicated by the spacing of the isobars and blowing parallel to them. The actual wind is deflected due to friction. Also, if the isobars are curved, then the wind speed is commonly somewhat less around low pressure and more around high pressure.

117 Cold air cascading down mountain slopes that come close to the sea.

118 Anabatic wind.

119 Squalls.

120 1805.

121 Rear Admiral Sir Francis Beaufort.

122 He was a noted surveyor, and served with distinction as Hydrographer of the Navy from 1829–55.

123 Force 5.

124 Fresh breeze. 17–21 knots.

125 Hurricane force.

126 A Bailey.
     B Viking.
     C Sole.
     D South East Iceland.
     E Trafalgar.

Winds of the World

127 (a) The Mistral.
     (b) From the Latin 'magistral', meaning the 'master wind'.
     (c) Off the Rhône River between Languedoc and Provence.

128 The Sirocco (also spelt Scirrocco).

129 The Leveche.

130 Off the coast of Argentina and Uruguay.

Clouds

131 (a) Cumulus.
     (b) Altostratus.
     (c) Stratus.
     (d) Cirrostratus.
     (e) Altocumulus.
     (f) Cumulonimbus.
     (g) Cirrocumulus.
     (h) Stratocumulus.
     (i) Nimbostratus.
     (j) Cirrus.

132 Thunder cloud (Cb) rises to great altitudes in the shape of an anvil.

133 Cumulus, congestus or towering.

134 Unsettled and windy weather.

135 Stratus fractus.

136 (a) A Depression or 'low' is a cyclone in extra tropical latitudes in which pressure can vary between 920 and 1020 millibars. The diameter of the depression can be anything from 100 to 2000 miles and is associated with unsettled weather, rain and gales. The system may be slow moving or travel up to 50 knots. Depressions often have fronts linked with them and may well come in a 'family' of four or five.

(b) An occlusion is a front which develops in the latter stages of the life cycle of a frontal depression. The cold front travels faster than the warm front, eventually overtaking it. The warm sector between the two is then lifted off the surface and the fronts are said to be 'occluded'. Occlusions can be cold or warm, depending on the relative temperatures of the cold air mass on either side.

137 The pressure is rising through it.

138 By moving or extending north-east!

Can You Complete?

139 Short notice, soon past. Another version is:

Long notice, long past,
Short notice, short past.

140 . . . prepare for a blow.
. . . lofty canvas you may fly.

141 . . . a careless ass. Another version is:

A greying sky and falling glass,
Soundly sleeps a careless ass.

142 . . . is a sailor's delight.
. . . in the morning is a sailorman's warning.

143 . . . make lofty ships carry low sails.

144 . . . for back it will run.

145 . . . oft foretells a stronger blow.

146 Shoot your lines, nets and trawl.

2 NAVIGATION

The Practice of Navigation

1 Lead. A careful watch on soundings.
  Log. Keeping the reckoning.
  Lookout. Keeping a careful lookout by all available means.
2 The navigator introduces a deliberate bias in the course so that there will be no doubt as to which side of a mark he will make his landfall.
3 The LOP is transferred to pass through the island. The navigator then 'aims off' to one side of the island until he can sail along the transferred LOP.
4 Assuming the coast is lit, the best time in general is pre dawn so that the ship's position can be fixed by bearings of lights. As day breaks, other marks may be identified by 'shooting up' from a known position.
5 As the ship increases her west longitude, or decreases her east longitude, the clocks used to keep ship's time are retarded one hour for every 15° of longitude as the ship proceeds from one time zone to the next. On crossing the 180th meridian, the date is advanced by twenty-four hours. The ship appears to lose a day. The chronometer is never altered. It keeps GMT.
6 (a) Time azimuth.
  (b) By comparison with another compass, eg the gyro.
  (c) Transits.
  (d) Bearings of a distant mark from a known position.
  (e) Finding the magnetic bearing of a distant object from an unknown position by taking the mean of several compass bearings taken on equidistant headings. The compass bearings are then compared with the magnetic bearings.
  (f) Reciprocal bearings taken from a 'non magnetic' boat.
  (g) Use of the parallel index on a stabilised radar display.
  (h) By sun or moon amplitude.
7 By range and bearing from a conspicuous navigational mark or marks.
8 Date of survey. Date of latest edition, large corrections and small corrections. Density and regularity of soundings with respect to the type of seabed. Contour lines. No unsurveyed coastline (indicated by pecked line).

9 A light which can be seen at the instant it rises above the horizon, or which disappears suddenly as it dips below the horizon. The range of the light at this instant can be found from 'Rising or Dipping Distance Tables', or the 'Geographical Range Table' in the *Admiralty List of Lights*. The tables are entered with height of light against height of eye. Abnormal refraction will affect the distance, but an approximate position may be obtained combining the geographical range with a bearing of the light.

10 The navigation should be undertaken when the sun is behind the navigator and the water is rippled by a gentle breeze. The coral heads show as green patches in an otherwise blue sea. The observer should station himself as high as practicable.

Tools of the Trade

11 (a) Dutchman's log. A piece of wood is thrown overboard and the speed is calculated from the time taken to pass a measured distance on the ship.

(b) Common log, chip log or ship log. A development of the above. A piece of line was attached to the triangular wooden chip. A series of knots were tied in the line so that the number of knots counted over a given period of time represented the speed in nautical miles per hour, or 'knots' (hence the unit of speed).

(c) Towed log, taffrail log or patent log. A rotator is towed through the water at the end of a braided line and distance run through the water is recorded by a mechanical register. Speed may also be obtained by timing the number of revolutions in a given time.

(d) Impeller log. The impeller is normally mounted below the ship's hull. It contains a magnet which generates small electrical pulses in a coil which are then amplified. This log measures distance in the fore and aft line of the ship. Speed may also be obtained.

(e) Pitot log. This is another hull-mounted log which measures speed through the water in the ship's fore and aft line as a function of the dynamical water pressure created by the ship's forward motion. Distance may also be obtained.

(f) Electromagnetic log. An electromagnet is mounted on the ship's bottom which creates a magnetic field in the sea water. The motion of the ship causes an electric current to flow in the sea water. The resulting voltage is detected by a pair of contacts and amplified to give speed through the water in the fore and aft line. Distance may also be found.

(g) Doppler log. This makes use of the principle of the doppler shift to measure speed. The log may be either single axis or dual axis, sea track or ground track. In the single axis mode, the log reads speed in the fore and aft line of the ship. In the dual axis mode, speed is measured both fore and aft and athwartships. On ground track, the log records speed over the ground, assuming a 'bottom return'. Distance can also be found.

(h) Strain gauge log. This type of log measures speed through the water in the fore and aft line.

12 Flinders bar. This corrects for vertically induced magnetism in vertical soft iron in the fore and aft line of the ship – the iron terminating at the same level as the compass.

The spheres. These correct for induced magnetism in symmetrical horizontal soft iron. They also produce a certain amount of vertically induced magnetism at the compass.

Vertical magnets. These correct heeling error.

Fore and aft horizontal magnets. These correct the ship's fore and aft permanent magnetic field at the compass position.

Athwartships horizontal magnets. These correct the ship's permanent magnetic field at the compass position.

13 Integral control applies permanent helm automatically. It over-rides the manual setting. Derivative control applies helm as a function of the rate at which the ship's heading is changing.

14 The error is caused by the false rate of tilting experienced by the gyro due to the north/south component of the ship's velocity. The east/west component is normally ignored as it has little effect in practice. The error varies directly as the ship's speed and cosine of the course, and inversely as the latitude.

15 Make sure you search for soundings starting at the lowest

phase setting. Multiple echoes may otherwise be mistaken for actual soundings.

16 Echo sounders are calibrated for an assumed speed of propagation of sound in sea water of 1,500mps. The Red Sea has high temperature combined with high salinity. This causes an increase in the speed of propagation of the sound pulse. The indicated depth will, therefore, be less than the actual depth.

17 (a) A straight line.

(b) A curve which spirals towards the pole, (unless the course is due east or west, in which case it will be following a parallel of latitude, or north/south, in which case it would be a meridian).

18 The ground wave signal may be contaminated by sky wave signals.

19 Vertical metal structures, masts, rigging, etc, rising above the base of the loop aerial may cause 'site error' (or 'semicircular error') which is frequency sensitive. It may be insignificant at 300kHz, but relatively large at higher frequencies.

20 (a) Index mirror not perpendicular to the plane of the sextant.

(b) Horizon mirror not perpendicular to the plane of the sextant.

(c) Horizon mirror not parallel to the index mirror when the sextant is set at 0°.

Nautical Astronomy

21 By identifying the Plough. The two stars at the front of the Plough point in the direction of the Pole Star which lies about five times their distance away.

The true altitude of the Pole Star is very nearly equal to the latitude of the observer. The observer may set his own latitude on the sextant, point the sextant due north and he should then see the Pole Star in the sextant telescope.

22 A star is said to be circumpolar for a particular observer when it never sets below the horizon. For a star to be circumpolar the latitude of the observer must be not less than the star's polar distance (90° 'minus declination'). They must be in the same hemisphere.

Alioth would be just circumpolar in latitude 34° north.

23 Index error. Dip. Refraction. Parallax. Semi diameter.

24 Sirius (magnitude minus 1.6). It is in the constellation of Canis Major, the large hunting dog of Orion, and can be located to the south-east of Orion's belt.

25 Venus, Mars, Jupiter and Saturn. The value adopted in the *Nautical Almanac* for the hourly change of GHA of the sun and planets is 15° 00'.0. The planets have a slightly greater rate than this and the tabulated 'v' correction represents the average hourly discrepancy on a certain day. The correction is, therefore, normally added to GHA. In the case of Venus, the correction becomes negative when Venus has a very high direct motion at superior conjunction.

26 The difference between Mean time and Apparent time. It is tabulated in the *Nautical Almanac*, but is no longer used in practical navigation.

27 The earth's spin axis 'wobbles' slightly in a period of 26,000 years. This causes the first point of Aries to precess in a retrograde motion along the ecliptic at 50".2 per year. This is known as 'precession of the equinoxes'. Lunar forces cause additional precession having a period of nineteen years known as 'nutation'.

28 The interval between two successive new moons. It is equal to 29½ days.

29 Civil twilight. Star sights may normally be taken when the sun is between 3° and 9° below the horizon. The mean of these two values is represented by the time of civil twilight when the sun is 6° below the horizon.

30 The sun rises bearing due east and sets bearing due west whenever its declination is 0°, ie at the vernal and autumnal equinoxes.

Electronic Aids

31 In the so called 'catch rain position', ie with one of the reflectors facing upwards.

32 A radar responder beacon which transmits a pulse upon reception of an interrogating pulse from a ship's radar. The pulse may be coded for identification purposes and will show intermittently as a flash on the radar screen of the observing ship radiating from the position of the racon.

33 The heading marker is not firing at the instant the centre of the radar beam sweeps across the ship's head. It may be adjusted by a small switch in the scanner unit.

34 The area between two navigational hyperbolae of zero phase difference is called a 'lane'. The distance between two such hyperbolae on the base line is equal to half the wavelength at the phase comparison frequency. This distance increases as the receiver moves away from the base line. This phenomena is known as 'lane expansion'.

In the Omega system, 'lane expansion' is small due to the very large base line length compared with the wavelength. The curvature of the earth also minimises the effect.

In the Decca Navigator system the wavelength, although shorter than that used for Omega, is comparatively large with respect to the base line.

Omega: half wavelength, 8 nautical miles; base line 5,000 or so nautical miles.

Decca: half wavelength, ¼ nautical mile; base line 120 or so nautical miles.

35 To eliminate the effect of ionospheric refraction in a dual channel Sat-Nav receiver. Most marine receivers are only single channel.

36 Short-term skywaves cannot arrive earlier than 35 microseconds after the beginning of the pulse. A sampling (or index) point is chosen at the end of the third cycle eg at the 30 micro-seconds point.

37 Relative display: ship's head up; course up; and north up. These may be centred or off-centred.

True motion: sea stabilised; ground stationed; and situation display.

38 If the stations transmitted at the same frequency, they could not be identified at the receiver. To overcome this problem, the stations transmit continuously at different frequencies, each frequency being a multiple of 14kHz.

The Master Station transmits at 6×14kHz; 'Red slave' at 8×14kHz, 'Green slave' at 9×14kHz, and then 'Purple slave' at 5×14kHz. In the receiver, the master signal is compared with each slave signal at the lowest common multiple of their two frequencies Thus:

	Comparison frequency
Master and Red slave	24 × 14kHz
Master and Green slave	18 × 14kHz
Master and Purple slave	30 × 14kHz.

39 A doppler radar makes use of the doppler shift principle to measure the speed of approach of a ship. They are often used when berthing very large ships when the speed of approach onto the berth may be critical.

40 (a) Plan position indicator.
  (b) Automatic radar plotting aid.
  (c) Sudden ionospheric disturbance.
  (d) Centicycles.
  (e) Line of position.
  (f) Ship's inertial navigation system.

3 RACING

Around the Marks

1 Yes. If your anchor is over the line at the start you will be counted as a premature starter.

2 At the moment you begin your manoeuvre to return, eg easing sheets in order to slow down.

3 No. Once you are back on the pre-start side of the line you get back your rights but you cannot use them immediately. You must allow boats over which you have right of way 'ample room and opportunity to keep clear'. In this case your opponent has the choice of either hitting the buoy or you, so he must be given room.

4 Yes. The 'I' flag normally means that premature starters must sail round either end of the line in order to restart. It will be hoisted usually one minute before the start. The race committee have probably made an error in lowering the warning and preparatory flags, but you start on the visual signal. Starting signals will often vary from race to race, so a sound signal is made to draw attention to the visual signal.

   If you are new to this particular race make sure you read your sailing instructions carefully before the race begins. In the above case you could argue with the race committee when the race is over.

5 No. Assuming that in this race, the 720° turn rule applies, while doing penalty turns you have no rights over any other boats.

6 When you are close-hauled and decide to go about you are luffing from the moment you begin the manoeuvre until your boat is directly head to wind. Once the boat's head has passed the eye of the wind you are tacking and remain so until your boat is close-hauled on the new track.

7 No. There is no obligation to call 'starboard', but if you often do this manoeuvre a few lengths away from a port tack boat you are likely to become unpopular!

8 No. You've left it too late. The shore counts as a continuous obstruction, but only when you call for room well before tacking can you make starboard tack boats go about. Otherwise you will have go aground to avoid infringing the port-starboard rule. (An interesting and surprising fact. Most of us would avoid going aground, put the boat about, throw the starboard tack boats into a 'B's' muddle and argue the point later!)

9 No. For boats on opposite tacks rounding a windward mark, the rules apply as though the boats were in open waters.

10 Yes. In open water the port and starboard rule applies even in an overtaking situation.

11 Yes. A boat can finish correctly when capsized, but all her crew must be aboard and the tide must do the work. You are not allowed to swim the capsized boat to the finishing line.

12 No, his spinnaker must be deemed to be in its normal position for that point of sailing.

NOTE

Interpretation of the racing rules is notoriously a subject for argument and 'protest'. If in doubt, please consult *The Rules Book* by Eric Twiname carefully!

The America's Cup

13 Around the Isle of Wight on Friday 22 August 1851.

14 The Royal Yacht Squadron One Hundred Guinea Cup was

renamed the America's Cup after the winner of that first race, and not because the United States have never lost it. It is the world's oldest International trophy.

15 A dispute arose over an interpretation of the race rules concerning whether the Nab Tower, a mark of the course, should have been left to port or starboard. Under present America's Cup rules, the yacht would also have been disqualified for not carrying a wholly national crew, having recruited some sailors in Cowes for the race.

16 Queen Victoria on seeing the race from the Royal Yacht.

17 Bolted to the floor of the New York Yacht Club's Manhattan mansion.

18 The head of the helmsman who loses it!

19 Twenty-four.

20 Eight and seventy-eight!

21 Sir Thomas Lipton, the grocer millionaire who between 1899 and 1930 challenged five times with his yachts, each one called *Shamrock*. The closest he came to winning was in 1920, when *Shamrock IV* lost 2–3 to *Resolute* in the best of five series off New York.

22 Sir T. O. M. Sopwith with *Endeavour* in 1934, who lost 2–4, in a series which some say should have gone the other way.

23 On a technicality, the New York Yacht Club committee refused to hear a protest lodged by the British. At the time *Endeavour* had a 2–1 lead and had beaten *Rainbow* in the fourth race.

24 'England rules the waves, America "waives" the Rules.'

25 $$\frac{L + 2d + SA - F}{2.37}$$

Broadly speaking, L = length, d is a girth dimension, SA is the rated sail area, and F is the average of three freeboard measurements. The 12 Metre Rule also incorporates other limitations such as minimum beam (11.8ft), maximum draft (9.5ft), mast height (82ft) and jib stay height (75% of mast height).

26 Sir Peter Scott.

27 John Oakeley was dismissed and he was replaced by Laurie Smith during the preliminary races.

28 Dennis Conner helmed *Freedom* to victory.

29 Jim Hardy helmed *Australia*.

30 An extremely bendy mast, which improved air flow, provided increased sail area, and gave a distinct advantage in light airs. The Australians won a race in conditions such as these, but there had been insufficient time to tune and develop the rig for heavier winds. The mast had been stepped one week before the first challenge race!

31 The Lipton Cup is presented by the Royal Ulster Yacht Club, who hold the trophy in their clubhouse at Bangor, Co. Down, in memory of Sir Thomas Lipton, whose challenges were issued through the Royal Ulster.

32 Three yachts have returned to defend their own victory. *Columbia* beat *Shamrock* in 1899 and *Shamrock II* in 1901; *Intrepid* beat *Dame Pattie* in 1967 and *Gretel II* in 1970; and *Courageous* beat *Southern Cross* in 1974 and *Australia* in 1977.

Racing and Cruising Milestones

33 In 1661, when Charles II and the Duke of York raced their yachts between Greenwich and Gravesend for a wager of £100. The king lost on the outward run, but won on the way back.

34 The X One designs. There are about 160 still racing on the south coast of England at several yachting centres, including Cowes, Itchenor, the Hamble and Poole Harbour. The first boat was designed by Alfred Westmacott of the Isle of Wight and was built in 1909 for less than £50.

35 The International Fourteen Dinghy.

36 Stewart H. Morris. He won the annual Prince of Wales Cup race, the principal British championship trophy in the class, from 1932 to 1936, from 1947 to 1949, in 1957, from 1960 to 1962 and in 1965.

37 Edward Heath.

38 Uffa Fox.

39 Arthur Ransome.

40 11 July 1903, from the Royal Cork Yacht Club to Glanmuire, Ireland. It was a race for power-boats of 40ft or under. The winner was *Napier Minor*, 40ft, with a 75hp Napier engine and driven by Campbell Muir.

41 1925, when just seven yachts started. The race was won by *Jolie Brise*.

42 In 1968 she became the smallest yacht ever to make an ocean crossing. She was just 5ft 11½in in length and was sailed by Hugo S. Vihlen from Casablanca to Fort Lauderdale between 29 March and 21 June 1968.

43 Robin Knox-Johnston who left Falmouth, Cornwall, in his 32ft Bermudan ketch, *Suhaili*, on 14 June 1968, and arrived back there, without having touched land, on 22 April 1969.

44 Anne Davison, in her 23ft sloop, *Felicity Ann*. She sailed from Plymouth to Miami between May 1952 and August 1953. Mrs Davison had previously been wrecked in another craft off Portland Bill, on her way to the West Indies with her husband, Frank. Tragically, he died of exposure, but Anne managed to struggle ashore, mostly in the dark, and with great courage resolved to sail on alone. Having at last safely arrived in the USA, she settled there and married an American.

45 Colonel H. G. 'Blondie' Hasler, famous for his command of the Royal Marines' ('Cockleshell Heroes') raid on enemy shipping up the Gironde in World War II.

46 Chay Blyth and Rob James in the John Shuttleworth-designed 65ft trimaran, *Brittany Ferries GB*. They broke the east-to-west sailing record (15 days, 20 hours, which has stood since 1824), by reaching Newport in 14 days, 13 hours and 54 minutes.

47 They achieved the longest survival in peace-time, and incidentally the longest in an inflatable raft or dinghy, when their yacht *Auralyn* was sunk by sperm whales north east of the Galapagos Islands in the Pacific on 4 March 1973. They drifted for 118 days until rescued by a Korean fishing boat on 30 June. During the period the couple were adrift, they sighted no less than seven ships. But none of the vessels, even though some came as close as half a mile, appeared to see the two survivors frantically trying to attract their attention.

4 THE QUEEN'S NAVEE

Great Sea Battles and Ships

Battles

1 William of Normandy to conquer England in 1066.
2 Sir Francis Drake on the day he entered Cadiz in 1587 to 'singe the King of Spain's beard'.
3 Nelson. After the Battle of the Nile on 1 August 1798 when, by way of reward, the King of Naples conferred upon him an estate in Sicily named Bronté. Nelson took great pride in this and afterwards signed himself 'Nelson and Bronté'.
4 Kentish Knock (1653). Solebay (1672). Quiberon Bay (1759). The Saints (1782). The Glorious First of June (1749). The North Cape (1943).

Kentish Knock (1653). This was a battle between the Dutch and the English in the Thames Estuary. Blake's attack won the day and enabled Cromwell to send his ships safely into the North Sea and Western Approaches on convoy escort duty.

Solebay (or *Southwold Bay*) (1672). The Anglo-French fleet under the command of the Duke of York fought the Dutch fleet under de Ruyter. The battle brought tactical success to the Dutch, though it was a hard fought action in which there were over 4,000 casualties.

Quiberon Bay (1759). This was a brilliant victory in a storm in which Hawke chased the French fleet, under Conflans, into the dangerous waters off the Brittany coast and destroyed seven ships for the loss of two.

The Saints (or *Dominica*) (1782). Thirty-six British ships, under Rodney, successfully fought the French (thirty-one ships) under de Grasse. There were over 3,000 casualties, the French admiral being killed.

Glorious First of June (1794). Four hundred miles west of Ushant, twenty-six British ships under Howe, met an equally strong French fleet, under Villaret-Joyeuse. There were over 8,000 casualties in this nominally British victory, though the grain convoy the French were screening succeeded in getting into Brest.

The Battle of the North Cape (1943). While trying to attack

a convoy, the German battle cruiser, *Scharnhorst*, was intercepted by British ships under Fraser. After a gallant struggle
in darkness and heavy weather, *Scharnhorst* was sunk by a
hail of radar-controlled gunfire and several hits by torpedoes.

5 The two penny piece which carries the Prince of Wales'
feathers. The Black Prince, who was the Prince of Wales,
gained the feathers at Crécy in 1346. He also fought at the
Battle of 'Les Espanols sur Mer'; and the Jutland casualty was
the armoured cruiser, The *Black Prince*, which was sunk by
the Germans in 1916 with the loss of nearly 900 men.

6 The Battle of Lepanto in 1571; one of the greatest naval
battles of history, in which the Spanish and Venetians fought
the Turks. The battle was especially significant in having
been the last major clash involving galleys. Miguel de
Cervantes, of course, was the author of *Don Quixote*.

7 The Battle of Chesapeake Bay in 1781, in which the British,
under Graves, were outmanoeuvred by the French, under de
Grasse, who took possession of the Bay, thus cutting off
communications with General Cornwallis who was forced to
surrender at Yorktown.

8 The *Director* at the Battle of Camperdown off the Dutch
coast in 1797, in which the British fleet defeated the Dutch.
    The *Glatton* at the Battle of Copenhagen in 1801, in which
Nelson defeated the Danes.

9 At the Battle of Navarino Bay in 1827.

10 On 19 December 1941, Italian frogmen, using 'chariots',
(two-man human torpedoes) planted limpet mines on the two
British battleships HMS *Valiant* and HMS *Queen Elizabeth*
and damaged them severely. The frogmen also damaged
other ships.

11 *Roma*. On 9 September 1943, after the Italians had
surrendered, units of their fleet were steaming for Allied
ports. The battleship *Roma*, with other heavy units, was
attacked by German aircraft west of Corsica and was hit by a
radio-controlled glider bomb. A fierce fire started and after
twenty minutes the ship blew up with heavy loss of life. The
battleship *Italia* was also hit but survived the attack.

12 (a) The code name given to the assault phase of 'Operation
Overlord' (the general plan for the liberation of Europe in
June 1944) in which the Navy played the major role.

(b) The evacuation from Dunkirk in May and June 1940.

(c) The invasion of Sicily in July and August 1943.

(d) The attack on the German battleship, *Tirpitz*, by midget submarines in September 1943.

(e) The invasion of North Africa in November 1942 to February 1943.

(f) The German code word for the projected invasion of Great Britain.

(g) The German invasion of Norway and Denmark.

(h) The Royal Marines ('Cockleshell Heroes') attack on German shipping at Bordeaux in December 1942.

(i) The raid on Dieppe in August 1942.

(j) A heavily escorted convoy for the relief of Malta in August 1942.

Ships

13 The USS *Constitution* which was launched in 1797. She is still afloat in the navy yard at Boston where she was built.

14 Britain's first nuclear submarine, *Dreadnought*, was launched on Trafalgar Day, 21 October 1960.

15 (a) She was the flagship of Lord Howard of Effingham who commanded the English fleet in the fighting against the Armada.

(b) *Ark Raleigh*, because she was ordered to be built by Sir Walter Raleigh. He later sold his fine new ship to the Queen and the vessel was thus renamed *Ark Royal*. She subsequently became *Anne Royal*.

(c) She was torpedoed and sunk in the Mediterranean by U-81 in 1941.

(d) Rod Stewart. 'Sailing'.

(e) Trafalgar.

(f) Bismarck.

16 She was the first vessel to use steam propulsion for commercial purposes. Launched on the Clyde in 1802, she was propelled by a stern paddle wheel and demonstrated her usefulness by towing two lighters on a canal for a distance of 20 miles. Local authorities, fearing that the canal banks would be damaged by this new form of vessel forbade its use.

17 (a) Admiral Sir Clowdisley Shovel (or Shovell).

(b) The Scilly Islands.

(c) The *Association*. Relics from the ship are still being recovered.

18 In May 1845 the steam-sloop *Rattler* fitted with a screw was attached, stern to stern, with the similar shaped steam-sloop *Alecto*, fitted with paddles. Having in previous tests shown herself far superior to the *Alecto*, the *Rattler* then proceeded to tow the *Alecto* backwards at the rate of 2½ knots!

19 HMS *Caroline*. Built in 1914, the *Caroline* formed a unit of the 1st Light Cruiser Squadron and is now the RNR drillship at Belfast.

20 The aircraft carrier HMS *Courageous*. She was torpedoed by a German U-boat, U-29, in the Western Approaches.

21 (a) Admiral Graf Spee.
(b) The River Plate.
(c) HMS *Ajax*, HMS *Exeter* and HMS *Achilles*.

22 The cruiser HMS *Edinburgh*, which had the same profile as HMS *Belfast*; the foremost funnel not being in the bridge structure as in the others of the class but stepped further aft, made them less attractive to a sailor's eye. The *Edinburgh* was sunk in the Barents Sea, north of Murmansk, in April 1942. She was carrying Russian gold to pay war debts. The *Belfast* is now moored in the Thames near Tower Bridge.

23 The *Admiral Scheer*. The *Jarvis Bay*.

24 The *Californian*. Her captain, Stanley Lord, was accused of not coming to the aid of the sinking liner, though subsequent evidence cleared him of blame. 1,490 lives were lost in the disaster.

Flags and Signals

The Royal Yacht

25 HM the Queen.

26 The Royal Standard from the mainmast, the Lord High Admiral's flag from the foremast and the Union flag from the mizzen.

27 They disappear down the funnel! (It is a false funnel, of course, inside the main structure, where a signalman is on duty to collect the flags and stow them.)

28 Always.

29 Because King George V once left his own link button out

when dining with the officers on board, who subsequently removed their own and have left them out up to the present day.

30 Provided that he is recommended, until he leaves the Navy. The current coxswain has served on board HMY *Britannia* since the ship was built.

31 Rear-Admiral. His title is Flag Officer Royal Yachts and he is the only admiral in the navy to have command of a ship.

32 From when the Yacht was first commissioned in January 1953.

33 The Yachtsmen have two short ribbons hanging from the back of their waistband as was the old custom in the navy.

34 Never. Only the Queen is piped aboard, although other dignitaries and foreign royalty may receive this honour with Her Majesty's personal approval.

35 When proceeding abaft the funnel in acknowledgment of entering the royal section of the ship.

36 To carry a Rolls Royce for visits to countries that do not have a car suitable for Her Majesty.

Naval Tradition

37 When the last line loses contact with the shore.

38 The Royal Marine bugler is traditionally known in the navy as 'Sticks'.

39 Never!

40 A very long white pendant with a red St George's Cross in the hoist.

41 The 'gin pendant', which invites friends to come aboard for a drink.

42 A flag-lieutenant.

43 At midnight on New Year's Eve (eight bells for the old year, eight bells for the new).

44 The youngest officer, sailor or marine in the ship to ensure good luck. 'Benjamin'.

45 Because the noise could be confused with the piping of orders. It is also considered bad luck because of a belief that this will 'whistle up the wind', thereby bringing a storm.

46 A master-at-arms.

Flags

47 The German naval ensign. At a distance or in poor light, its design resembled that of the white ensign.

48 1 A (white and blue).
    2 G (yellow and blue).
    3 I (yellow and black).
    4 L (yellow and black).
    5 N (blue and white).
    6 Q (yellow)
    7 S (white and blue).
    8 U (red and white).
    9 W (blue, white and – in the middle – red).
   10 Z (black and – clockwise – yellow, blue and red).

49 The Union flag.

50 (a) I have a diver down; keep well clear at slow speed.
   (b) I require a pilot.
   (c) I am on fire and have dangerous cargo on board. Keep well clear of me.
   (d) You are running into danger.
   (e) Keep clear of me, I am manoeuvering with difficulty.
   (f) Man overboard.
   (g) I require assistance.
   (h) I require medical assistance.
   (i) I am dragging my anchor.
   (j) My engines are going astern.

51 The ensign must be fully hoisted *before* being 'dipped'.

52 On a halyard at the peak of the main.

53 (a) An ensign of smaller size for use in rough weather.
   (b) An extra large white ensign flown from the masthead when engaging the enemy. As a matter of interest, in World War I HM ships in action used a red ensign at the fore yardarm until just before Jutland (1916), when this was replaced by the Union flag.

54 Bunting-tosser, or 'Bunts'.

55 When in harbour, flying the flag of an Admiral of the Fleet, and with a court martial sitting onboard.

56 A crimson flag with gold horizontal anchor.

57 9 July 1864, when by an Order in Council it was directed that the classification of ships under the denominations of Red, White and Blue Squadrons should be discontinued. In

future, the white ensign was to be used by all HM ships of war in commission.

58 (a) Flew a 'Jolly Roger' flag.
   (b) Flew pendants from their periscopes for each ship sunk.

Morse code

59 (a) E = ·   (b) H = · · · ·   (c) K = — · —
   (d) M = — —   (e) N = — ·   (f) Q = — — · —
   (g) R = · — ·   (h) U = · · —   (i) W = · — —
   (j) Y = — · — —

60 Three.
61 What ship?

Signals with a Smile

62 '. . . we rely on skill!'
63 'Sex equality'.
64 'Snap!'
65 'Buy a farm!'
66 Because the sovereign is about to pass in the Royal Yacht and will receive a cheer from the ship's companies lining the decks of each vessel. 'Hip, hip, hooray!'
67 '20 knots!'

The 'Andrew' Lingo

68 Supposedly after Andrew Miller, an officer of the press-gang who 'pressed' so many men into the navy that he was said to have owned it!
69 Winston Churchill when First Lord of the Admiralty prior to the outbreak of World War I. A special allowance payed to seamen serving in small ships to compensate them for the discomforts thereof.
70 A sailor's expression for anything irregular or disorganised. Harry Tate was a music-hall comedian of the early 1900s who performed a hilarious sketch with an old motor car which never worked properly.

Naval Nicknames

71 (a) 'Dickie' Bird.

    (b) 'Nobby' Clark.

    (c) 'Nellie' Dean.

    (d) 'Taff' Evans.

    (e) 'Froggy' French.

    (f) 'Dodger' Long.

    (g) 'Pincher' Martin.

    (h) 'Dusty' Miller.

    (i) 'Spud' Murphy.

    (j) 'Pedlar' Palmer.

    (k) 'Brigham' Young.

    (l) 'Hookey' Walker.

    (m) 'Bob' Tanner.

    (n) 'Knocker' White.

    (o) 'Tug' Wilson.

Food and Drink to a Sailor

72 Because in early times, the fresh water quickly went bad and was virtually undrinkable.

73 A term applied in the navy to any form of porridge – originating from the days of the old wooden wallers, then an unpopular mixture of coarse oatmeal boiled in water and sweetened with molasses which was served up to sailors for breakfast.

74 In the days of 'hard tack' biscuits the young midshipmen used to knock the weevils out of their biscuits, then preserve them in pill-boxes to be specially fed up and trained for maggot races along the mess tables!

75 A joint of cooked meat resting on a mound of peeled potatoes.

76 Knives and forks. (These did not become official issue until 1907. Prior to that, a seaman was supplied with a spoon by the Admiralty.)

77 Herrings in tomato sauce.

78 Sardines!

79 The galley hand who peels the potatoes.

100 Nautical Terms and Expressions

1 On the side opposite to the wind. On the lee side.

2 A narrow plank of the hold lining (ceiling) which can be removed in order to ventilate the spaces between a vessel's ceiling and skin planking.

3 Tallow placed in the hollow at the base of a sounding lead which picks up samples of the sea bottom.

4 Stop. Hold fast.

5 A vessel is said to be 'on her beam ends' when lying on her side.

6 A protruding strake around a vessel's topsides to guard them from damage when mooring alongside.

7 In the old wooden ships, the 'devil' was a big deck seam near the gunwale. A man working between this and the water-line was in a precarious position.

8 A document acknowledging receipt onboard of cargo as described in the 'bill'.

9 In sailing ships the bitts were wooden bollards to which the end of the anchor cable was attached. When this was run out to the limit it was said to be nearing the bitter end.

10 A small iron solid fuel stove.

11 When a vessel at anchor lies at a dangerous angle to her cable.

12 To haul down a rope taut.

13 A man who has served for a long period in barracks or a shore establishment.

14 In the RN the boat of a flag-officer.

15 Retired from sea service.

16 Cancel the last order.

17 A headland with a broad, perpendicular face.

18 Name formerly given to men of the Royal Marines because of their superb physique.

19 Rumour.

20 The rounded finishing pieces laid on top of wooden bulwarks.

21 To haul up a sail with clew-lines and bunt-lines ready for furling.

22 The raised edging of a hatchway or other deck opening.

23 The pointed extremity of the conical trawl fishing net.

24 A marking buoy mainly used by fishermen.

25 Empty bottle. Like a marine, it has done its duty and is ready to serve again.

26 A small wooden box which used to be issued to seamen for their small personal effects. It was replaced by an attaché-case just before the last war.

27 A small hand-winch.

28 To grumble or grouse.

29 Pronounced 'dïssa' or 'dïsso'; the small gondola-type rowing boat, common in Malta.

30 To complain.

31 The device of the Missions to Seamen consisting of a white angel on blue background.

32 The foremost headsail when four headsails are used.

33 The rounded intersection of the stem with the keel.

34 A small boat employed to assist ships in and around harbours.

35 One who takes part in sailing races held in cold or frosty weather, or who goes sailing for pleasure despite wintry conditions.

36 A rumour (usually unfounded!), so-called because tradition has it that such rumours had their beginnings in the galley or cook-house!

37 The ornate gilt coverings which used to adorn the sterns of former men-of-war.

38 Soldiers, or 'pongos'.

39 The line of water ahead of a vessel through which she will pass. The opposite to the wake.

40 An undeserved telling off.

41 A coastguard.

42 A ring made of wire, rope or metal.

43 Devonport.

44 An upright, tapered cask used for storing salted meat.

45 A local, unlicensed pilot.

46 Stray rope ends hanging untidily in the rigging.

47 Defaulters; usually leading to stoppage of leave or a spell of extra work!

48 Temporary. As in jury mast which is a mast made up to replace a damaged one.

49 Cocoa.

50 A small anchor. Also the term applied to a Leading Seaman because he wears an anchor on his arm as a distinguishing badge.

51 Two strong vertical timbers fixed in the bows of a wooden sailing vessel between which the squared heel of the bowsprit is locked.

52 A strong easterly wind in the Mediterranean Sea.

53 Alternative name for the second dog watch 6–8pm.

54 A timber spa with rope lanyards at either end used as a fender.

55 The handle of an oar. Also, the reflection of a seamark's light in the sky.

56 The frayed edges of well worn clothing.

57 The official inventory of all cargo carried by a merchant vessel.

58 The crockery and utensils used in a mess.

59 The anchor.

60 A gale blowing from straight ahead.

61 The point at which a mooring line or cable passes through a fairlead and may chafe.

62 The bell sounded to call the watch below a quarter of an hour before a change of watches.

63 A hand-guard used by the sailmaker when hand sewing which enables him to push the needle through the canvas.

64 Joining a ship late, just as she is about to sail.

65 Social duties ashore. Associated with tea parties ashore with the ladies.

66 Slang name for the mud or a mudbank, used particularly when a yacht has gone aground, ie 'onto the putty'.

67 (a) The Supply Officer of a warship (derived from the word 'purser').
   (b) A candle.
   (c) A clasp knife.
   (d) Shoes.
   (e) A food stain on clothing.
   (f) Soap.

68 The senior WRNS officer.

69 To be on the list of defaulters, or in 'report'.

70 The gun fired on the morning of the day appointed for a court martial.

71 Short pendants for hauling down and securing the cringle of a reefed sail to the boom.

72 A shoulder built around a mast to support the inboard end of a boom.

73 Food. But the 'scran-bag' was a receptacle or place in a ship where loose clothing left lying about was placed, to be redeemed by the payment of a piece of soap or its equivalent in pence.

74 To shatter, break into numerous pieces.

75 A man always in trouble or mischief.

76 Articles of service uniform clothing issued to officers or men of the Royal Navy.

77 A shoe maker.

78 Slippery hitch; one that will pull away when strain is applied.

79 When applied to rope or cable it means to stop suddenly. Also applied to the snatch of an anchored vessel against her cable when riding to her anchor in a seaway.

80 Sailors' term for a kipper.

81 A platform built out from the side of a ship.

82 A naval shore establishment.

83 Refuse.

84 To retire from sea service.

85 A channel across or between shoals or spits.

86 In the Royal Navy, a man charged with the cleanliness of a compartment or 'flat'. Sometimes used as a shortened term for minesweeper.

87 New entry.

88 One composed of instruments not found in the normal band, eg mouth organ, comb and paper, jew's harp . . .

89 Long underwear.

90 To avoid duty, to malinger.

91 The toprail round the stern of a ship from quarter to quarter.

92 Small, oval shaped, meat pie (Cornish pasty in the West Country).

93 A horizontal stay between masts, nowadays mostly serving as a jackstay to support signal halyards and radio aerials.

94 A line of mooring buoys.

95 When two blocks of a tackle are brought so close together that no further movement is possible.

96 To be early. To act or arrive before the appointed time.

97 Extremely stupid!

98 The owner, or person in charge, of a wharf.

99 Ribs or brackets attached to the barrel of a windlass, winch drum or capstan to provide good grip for cables, wraps, etc.

100 To swing from side to side of a ship's desired course, caused by bad steering or difficult weather conditions.

5 SUBMARINES

General

1 As 'boats'.

2 'The trade'.

3 Robert Whitehead, in 1867.

4 The ideal state when a dived submarine's weight exactly equals the weight of water displaced, enabling it to remain stopped in perfect balance. (It is extremely difficult to achieve and almost never happens!)

5 Titanium.

6 The 750-ton Type VIIC, the standard German U-boat, (comparable with the British 'S' Class submarine) could fully submerge in under 40 seconds and in certain conditions even as little as 20 seconds.

The Beginnings

7 Admiral Earl St Vincent of Prime Minister Pitt.

8 Bushnell's *Turtle* made an abortive attack on HMS *Eagle* in New York Harbour on 6 September 1776.

9 The CSS *Hunley* sank the Union ironclad *Housatonic* in Charleston Harbour on 1 February 1864 during the American Civil War. In fact the *Hunley* was no more than a semi-submersible armed with a suicidal spar torpedo; the little craft was itself sunk by the explosion!

10 *Resurgam* had a similar Lamm steam-engine which ran on a residual head of steam without requiring the boiler to be heated continuously. The Rev George William Garrett, a Manchester curate.

11 The *Blanco Encalada* in April 1891, during the Chilean Revolutionary War.

12 John Philip Holland who left Ireland for America in 1873 with the aim of building submarines to destroy the massive British fleet and thereby (the theory was!) bring about Ireland's independence. In this he was supported and funded by the Fenian Society in the USA.

Submarine Successes

13 Two midget submarines, HMS *X6* (Lt D. Cameron VC) and HMS *X7* (Lt B. C. G. Place VC) crippled the 42,000-ton German battleship *Tirpitz* lying in Kaa Fjord and the 'Beast' was never again operational.

14 To sever Axis supply lines between Italy and North Africa. The submarine campaign contributed greatly to Rommel's collapse and it has been argued that it was the prime cause. Certainly Rommel's Chief of Staff acknowledged this.

15 USS *Nautilus*, the US Navy's first nuclear submarine, which made the passage from the Bering Strait to the Greenland Sea and passed through the Pole on Sunday 3 August 1958.

16 The USN submarine force had already destroyed the Japanese merchant fleet on which the islands of Japan were wholly dependant for the prosecution of the war.

17 The USS *England* in the Pacific in May 1944.

18 The *Shinano*, the 59,000-ton Japanese aircraft carrier, sunk on her maiden voyage by the USS submarine, *Archerfish*.

Escape

19 Wilhelm Bauer when his Brandtaucher sank by accident in Kiel Harbour in 1851. He 'persuaded' (using a large spanner) his two crewmen to equalise the pressure by flooding to enable the hatch to be opened.

20 She sank on trials in the Gareloch, Scotland, in January 1917, when ventilators had not been shut properly. This led to one of the most famous stories of submarine salvage and rescue. After nearly two and a half days trapped below, forty-seven survivors were brought out of a hole cut in the lifted bows of the submarine.

21 The rear door of a torpedo tube was opened when the bow cap was also open.

22 Because oxygen (far too late for many would-be escapees) was eventually found to be highly toxic under pressure.

23 *Pisces III*.

24 About 600ft in modern hooded immersion suits. However, Deep Submergence Rescue Vehicles (mini-submarines) can rescue crews, several men at a time, from sunken submarines

at far greater depths, say 2,000ft. The Rescue Vehicles clamp themselves, limpet-like, over the special escape hatches.

Not so Serious

25 Very rough! The 'bird bath' is a canvas screen and bath rigged to catch water pouring down the conning tower into the control room.
26 Three white mice to warn of petrol fumes which poisoned them well in advance of humans. The mice were part of the complement and were paid (for the trio) 1s a day!
27 Commander Richard Compton-Hall, MBE, now Director of the Royal Navy's submarine museum at HMS 'Dolphin', Gosport.
28 By getting the drill wrong in discharging 'the heads' to sea by high pressure air!
29 Scrambled eggs, tinned bacon and tomatoes for breakfast, eaten preferably in red lighting (for night vision) which mercifully robs the dish of colour.
30 'Scratch' is the submariner's somewhat irreverent nickname for the Second Coxswain.

6 SEA PERSONALITIES

Nelson Himself

1 (a) The Battle of Copenhagen, 1801.
  (b) 'Leave off action' which Nelson was given permission to do by the Commander-in-Chief, Admiral Sir Hyde Parker, at the hottest moment of the battle. The signal was intended to be permissive, though Nelson did not appreciate this.
2 (a) HMS *Agamemnon*, sixty-four guns. Commanded by Captain Horatio Nelson from 1793 to 1797.
  (b) Buckler's Hard on the Beaulieu River in Hampshire.
3 'Engage the enemy more closely.'
4 One who had worked his way up from the lower deck.
5 At the attack on Santa Cruz in 1797.

6 He was blinded by gravel thrown up by a cannon shot when the Royal Navy was besieging the citadel of Calvi, in Corsica.
7 Forms of shot.
8 *Neptune.*
9 The brilliant administrator, Lord Barham.
10 She died poverty stricken, in Calais, in 1815.
11 This was a term of contempt applied to soldiers or marines, because they wore red coats and were regarded by sailors as inferior.
12 The Battle of Cape St Vincent in 1797 where Nelson was supported by soldiers of the regiment when he boarded and captured two Spanish ships.

Sailors through History

13 The Duke of Medina Sidonia commanded the Spanish Armada, known to the Spanish as the Enterprise of England. The original commander was the Marquis of Santa Cruz who died in February 1588, the Armada sailing in May of that year.
14 Admiral Richard Kempenfelt.
15 Vice-Admiral Lord Cuthbert Collingwood.
16 On 12 February, the German battleships *Gneisenau* and *Scharnhorst*, with the cruiser *Prinz Eugen* and escorting vessels, left Brest and were not detected until passing the Dover Straits area. Both battleships were later damaged by mines in Dutch waters, but this Channel dash under the command of Vice-Admiral Ciliax was regarded as a success by the Germans and an embarrassing event by the British.
17 Kapitan Lothar von Arnauld de la Periere who in World War I sank or damaged 406,400 tons of Allied shipping.
18 Lieutenant Commander M. D. Wanklyn who, as commanding officer of HM Submarine *Upholder*, sank or damaged over 130,000 tons of Axis shipping, including two Italian submarines.
19 Admiral of the Fleet, the Earl Mountbatten of Burma.
20 Naomi James. First woman to sail single-handed round the globe via Cape Horn, and in the fastest time ever.
21 (a) King William IV.
   (b) 'The Sailor King'.

22 (a) The explorer, John Cabot.

(b) Sebastian Cabot.

23 Captain James Cook.

24 Bougainvillaea.

25 Admiral Edward Vernon.

26 Admiral John Byng. He was shot on the quarterdeck of the *Monarch* in Portsmouth Harbour. The story goes that he tied his own blindfold and gave his own signal to the firing squad by dropping a handkerchief.

27 Juan Sebastian del Cano who assumed command of the remnants of the original fleet when its leader met his tragic end.

28 The Portuguese navigator, Ferdinand Magellan. He was killed by natives in Mactan, an island of the Philippines, in April 1521.

29 Martin Frobisher.

30 Richard Jenkins. His ear. The War of Jenkins' Ear, 1739, which later developed into the War of the Austrian Succession, 1739–48.

31 Admiral Sir John Fisher. *Dreadnought.*

32 Francis Drake. Thomas Doughty.

33 Admiral David Beatty.

34 Clare Francis.

35 Adlard Coles, *Heavy Weather Sailing* and *Creeks and Harbours of the Solent* being among his most famous books.

36 Chay Blyth.

37 Uffa Fox.

38 Dame Agnes E. Weston, nicknamed 'Aggie' Weston.

39 Captain Joshua Slocum.

40 Sir Francis Chichester.

41 Dougal Robertson. *Lucette.* He told the incredible story of his family's survival in his book *Survive the Savage Sea.*

42 Captain O. M. Watts, founder of Reed's *Nautical Almanac,* and who has recently retired from his famous chandlery in London's Albemarle Street.

7 MUSIC MARITIME

Opera and Ballet

1 They all contain sea storms.

2 The retired merchant skipper in Benjamin Britten's opera, *Peter Grimes*.

3 The pirates, with 'cat-like tread' in Gilbert and Sullivan's *Pirates of Penzance*.

4 (a) *The Pearl Fishers*.
   (b) Bizet.
   (c) Zurga and Nadir.

5 (a) Used as the signature tune for the TV series *The Onedin Line*.
   (b) The ballet, *Spartacus*.
   (c) Khachaturian.

6 (a) *The Wreckers*.
   (b) Ethel Smyth.
   (c) Cornwall.

Music with a Salty Flavour

7 'King Neptune sat on his lonely throne' is one of the songs from Edward German's operetta *Merrie England*. Neptune is one of the planets in Gustav Holst's famous work, *The Planets*.

8 (a) Debussy.
   (b) *La Mer* ('The Sea').
   (c) *Jeux de Vagues* ('Play of the Waves') and *Dialogue du vent et de la mer* ('Dialogue of the wind and the sea').

9 (a) Vaughan Williams.
   (b) *A Sea Symphony*.
   (c) Walt Whitman.

10 Frederick Delius.

11 Sir Edward German.

12 Claude Debussy.

13 Sir Henry Wood.

14 (a) Sir Edward Elgar.
   (b) These are the opening words to the 'Slumber Song' in Elgar's cycle of five songs entitled *Sea Pictures*.

Snatches of Shanties

15 (a) 'What shall we do with the drunken sailor?'
(b) 'Blow the man down'.
(c) 'Shenandoah'.
(d) 'Rio Grande'.
(e) 'A-roving'.
(f) 'Leave her, Johnny, leave her'.

8 THE ROYAL CONNECTION

In Music

1 The occasion of the Royal performance along the Thames of Handel's *Water Music*:

'A City Company's barge was employed for the Music', reported the *Daily Courant* of July 19th, 1717, 'wherein were 50 instruments of all sorts, who play'd all the way from Lambeth the finest symphonies, compos'd express for the occasion.'

2 At the 1899 Norwich Festival, the famous singer, Dame Clara Butt, dressed as a mermaid, gave the first performance of Elgar's *Sea Pictures*. Soon after the Première, Dame Clara was commanded to perform the songs for Queen Victoria at Balmoral Castle.

3 The song, 'I am Monarch of the sea', sung by the Rt Hon Sir Joseph Porter, KCB, First Lord of the Admiralty, in Gilbert and Sullivan's *HMS Pinafore*. The song includes, of course, the famous chorus about his 'sisters and his cousins and his aunts'.

In History

4 HMS *King Alfred*, the old RNVR training establishment on the front at Hove, Sussex.
5 (a) Charles II, in 1664.
(b) They may march through the City of London with bayonets fixed, colours flying and band playing any time they please!

6 (a) Prince Albert Edward, Queen Victoria's son.

  (b) In 1848, at the age of seven, the young prince went with his mother and father on a cruise to the West Country and Channel Islands in the Royal Yacht. While aboard, a special sailor's suit was made for him by the ship's tailors.

7 (a) The Prince Regent, in 1811.

  (b) The prince introduced the custom that ladies should be allowed to perform the launching ceremony.

8 The Anglo-Saxon King Edgar.

9 (a) The Prince of Wales (later King George V).

  (b) Admiral.

10 King Alfred.

11 When the National Anthem is being played, the loyal toast is drunk standing up.

9 I NAME THIS SHIP

1 From the old practice of toasting prosperity to the ship in a silver goblet of wine and then casting it into the sea to prevent a toast of ill-intent being drunk from the same cup.

2 Because on one occasion a lady performing the ceremony missed her aim and the bottle struck and injured a spectator who subsequently sued the Admiralty for damages.

3 HMS *Nelson* and HMS *Rodney*.

4 That the captain of the boat's parent ship, eg HMS *Vanguard*, is aboard the boat coming alongside.

5 Because the ship's name has to fit onto the sailor's cap badge!

6 The *Great Eastern*, 18,914 tons, the iron transatlantic passenger liner designed by Isambard Kingdom Brunel and built by Scott, Russell & Co at Milwall, on the Thames. 692ft long and with a beam of over 82ft over her paddle boxes, she was the only vessel in the world with both paddle wheels and propeller. She had five funnels and carried a spread of 58,000 sq ft of sail on her six masts. She had a maximum speed of about 15 knots.

10 WHO WROTE?

1 Eric Twiname in his classic book on dinghy racing, *Start to Win* (publ. Adlard Coles).
2 David Garrick. *Heart of Oak*, which Garrick wrote in 1759 to celebrate the naval victories over the French at Lagos and Quiberon Bay, and also the battle of Quebec.
3 Ludovic Kennedy of his father, Captain Edward Coverley Kennedy, RN. (Quoted in *War at Sea* by John Winton, publ. Hutchinson.)
4 Sir Winston Churchill. (Also quoted in *War at Sea*.)
5 Robert Louis Stevenson in *Treasure Island*. Jim Hawkins.
6 Eric Newby in *The Last Grain Race* (publ. Secker & Warburg).
7 Eric Hiscock in *Cruising Under Sail* (publ. OUP). He circumnavigated the world with his wife, Susan, in *Wanderer III*. They later voyaged together to the Pacific in a larger yacht, *Wanderer IV*.
8 Colin and Rosemary Mudie. (Quoted from *Off Watch*, ed James Skellorn, publ. Granada.)
9 Erskine Childers. *The Riddle of the Sands*.
10 Samuel Pepys.
11 Nicholas Monsarrat. *The Cruel Sea* (publ. Cassell). HMS *Compass Rose*.
12 G. M. Trevelyan in his *History of England* (publ. Longman Group Ltd).

11 WHO SAID?

1 Lord Macaulay.
2 Sir Richard Grenville of HMS *Revenge* (in Tennyson's famous poem 'The Last Fight of the *Revenge*').
3 Admiral Collingwood.
4 The water rat to the mole in *The Wind in the Willows* by Kenneth Grahame (publ. Methuen).
5 Adolf Hitler.
6 Chaplain H. M. Forgy, USN, during the Japanese attack on Pearl Harbour, 7 December 1941.
7 Oliver Cromwell.

8 Admiral John Fisher, in reply to a criticism of Captain Percy Scott, *c*1908.
9 Samuel Johnson to James Boswell, 16 March 1759.
10 On 16 February 1940, the destroyer HMS *Cossack* intercepted a German supply tanker in Jossing Fjord, in Norway, and released 299 prisoners. The shout 'The navy's here' by the boarding party on finding the prisoners became a catch phrase in the Royal Navy and the basis of a popular wartime song.
11 John Paul Jones, captain of the USS *Bonhomme Richard* replying to a hail from HMS *Serapis*, asking if he had surrendered during the action off Flamborough Head, 23 September 1779. After a fierce fight, the *Serapis* surrendered, the *Bonhomme Richard* later sinking.
12 Napoleon, at Rochefort in 1815, after Waterloo.

12 SOME CLASSICAL CLIPPINGS

1 (a) Samuel Taylor Coleridge.
  (b) 'The Rime of the Ancient Mariner'.
  (c) 'To the Evening Star'.
2 'Dover Beach'.

> Begin, and cease, and then again begin,
> With tremulous cadence slow, and bring
> The eternal note of sadness in.

3 Sir John Betjeman. 'Delectable Duchy' (the poem being about Cornwall). (Quoted from *Collected Poems*, publ. John Murray.)
4 (a) 'The Shark'.
  (b) Lord Alfred Douglas. (Quoted courtesy of Edward Colman, Literary Executor.)
5 Henry Wadsworth Longfellow.
6 Tennyson. 'The Sailor Boy'.
7 John A. Glover-Kind.

> I do like to stroll along the Prom, Prom, Prom,
> Where the brass bands play
> Tiddely om pom pom!

So just let me be beside the seaside
I'll be beside myself with glee
And there's lots of girls beside,
I should like to be beside,
Beside the seaside!
Beside the sea!

8 Land's End. Bolerium (or Bellerium) is the old Roman name for the Land's End area of Cornwall.
9 (a) *Red Peppers*.
   (b) Sir Noel Coward.
10 'Drake's Drum'. Sir Henry Newbolt. (Quoted courtesy of Peter Newbolt.)
11 (a) Captain Henry Morgan and Captain William Kidd.
   (b) Jolly Roger . . . Spanish Main.
   (c) They were two of the most notorious buccaneers in the history of piracy. (Quoted from *A Parliament of Birds* by John Heath-Stubbs, publ. Chatto & Windus.)
12 Thomas Campbell. 'Ye Mariners of England!'
13 John Masefield in his poem, 'Posted as Missing'. (Quoted courtesy of the Society of Authors, for the Estate of John Masefield.)
14 James Thomson.
15 *Henry V* (the Chorus in the Prologue to Act III).
16 (a) HMS *Royal George*.
   (b) Kempenfelt.
17 Walter de la Mare. (Quoted from *Complete Poems*, publ. Faber.)
18 Miranda, in Shakespeare's *Tempest*.
19 (a) . . . Road-rail, pig lead,
          Fire-wood, iron-ware,
               and cheap tin trays.
   (b) 'Cargoes'. (Quoted courtesy of the Society of Authors, as above.)
20 D. H. Lawrence. (Quoted from the *Complete Poems*, publ. Heinemann, courtesy of Laurence Pollinger Ltd, for the Estate of Frieda Lawrence Ravagli.)

13 SEA MYSTERIES

1 (a) The *Mary Celeste*.
  (b) The *Dei Gratia*, a brigantine, also out of New York.
2 (a) The famous frogman, Commander 'Buster' Crabb, OBE, GM, RNVR.
  (b) Crabb had disappeared in mysterious circumstances while, it was said, he was inspecting the hull of the 12,000-ton Russian cruiser *Ordzhonikidze* which came to Portsmouth carrying Marshal Bulganin and Mr Kruschev for their visit to Britain in April 1956. Commander Crabb has never been seen since.
3 (a) The *Marlborough* was found on 13 November 1913, off Tierra del Fuego by the British ship *Johnston*.
  (b) She was a green ship, totally covered in seaweed and mould. Scattered around her decaying decks lay gruesome skeletons, all that remained of her crew, and in the hold were the bones of sheep.
4 (a) The Prince of Wales, later to become George V.
  (b) The famous phantom ship, *The Flying Dutchman*.
5 (a) Sir John Franklin.
  (b) To discover the North-West Passage.
6 Atlantis.

14 CREATURES AT SEA

Half a Name

1 (a) Catwalk.
  (b) Cowhitch.
  (c) Crowsnest.
  (d) Doghouse.
  (e) Dogwatch.
  (f) Dolphin-striker.
  (g) Donkey's breakfast.
  (h) Gooseneck.
  (i) Horse Latitudes.
  (j) Monkey island.
  (k) Pig iron.
  (l) Ratlines.
  (m) Staghorn.
  (n) Dog star.
  (o) Monkey's fist.

Birds of the Feathered Variety

2 (a), (b) and (c) usually on rocky or cliff-lined coasts.
3 Phalarope.
4 From late spring to early autumn.
5 Any congregation of ocean birds sitting on the water.
6 Wagtail.
7 Sanderling.
8 Ruff is the male, reeve the female of the same species.
9 The cormorant is much larger, has white on the head and flank in breeding season, and a bronze coloured back. It is plentiful off rocky coasts or estuarine areas and even inland on fresh water.
  The shag is much smaller, and is black with a green sheen. It carries a tall crest in the breeding season and is associated with rocky coasts.
10 (a) Snipe.   (e) Teal.
   (b) Dunlin.   (f) Wild swans.
   (c) Wild geese.   (g) Widgeon.
   (d) Wild geese.
11 A 'pen'.
12 A seaslater is not a bird at all, but a marine isopod related to a woodlouse.
13 Storm petrels of any genus.

15 QUIZ FROM ALL QUARTERS

1 Colonel.
2 Area of supposed wave disturbance where the deep Atlantic gives place to the Continental Shelf approaching the English Channel.
3 A Viking chief at death used to be placed aboard his ship and surrounded by his needs for a voyage. The ship was then set aflame and sent to sea to burn out or sink.
4 Scrimshaw.
5 The point in the moon's orbit where it is nearest the earth.
6 31 July 1970.
7 A method used by bargemen for controlling their vessel going down river by dragging a length of chain along the

bottom, thus gaining steerage way to keep the barge in the channel.

8 55,623,900sq miles.
9 A waxy substance found in the head of a sperm whale. It was used in lubricating oils and industrial detergents, but because of limitations imposed on whaling, substitutes for spermaceti have had to be found.
10 'In irons'.
11 A sternboard.
12 The Spaniard, Vasco Nunez de Balboa when he marched across the Isthmus of Darien in 1513 and saw the waters of the Pacific from a peak of the mountain range which runs down the Isthmus.
13 Lord Kitchener and his staff were taking passage to Russia when HMS *Hampshire* struck a mine and sank in 15 minutes with the loss of all but a handful of her complement.
14 HMS *Beagle*.
15 Ferdinand de Lesseps.
16 Master under God.
17 He allows a rope or warp under strain to slip slightly round a capstan or bollard, but still under control.
18 To alter course with the wind almost astern to bring the wind onto the other quarter (in fore-and-aft rig yachts, to 'gybe').
19 Balls of light (associated with an electrical storm) which can form on a ship's mast or rigging.
20 The predominantly westerly winds in southern latitudes, between around 40°S and 50°S, which can cause tempestuous seas and storms, eg around Cape Horn.
21 A boy employed in battle in the old men-o-war to keep the muzzle loading guns supplied with powder from the magazine.
22 Before a sea battle hammocks were rolled up and lashed to the ship's gunwales (or placed in nettings along the gunwales) to afford some protection against flying splinters and musket fire from the enemy.
23 The destroyer HMS *Hampshire*.
24 A bay in the Galapagos Islands where whalers on long voyages picked up and left letters to and from home in a barrel.
25 The world's greatest archipelago is the crescent of over

13,000 islands straddling the equator that forms Indonesia.

26 The tops of the doors in the superstructure of the *Sir Winston Churchill* are rounded; those of the *Malcolm Miller* are square.

27 It is an ice-free port situated in North West Russia; destination of the arctic convoys during World War II. Ice free because it has the benefit of the last flick of the Gulf Stream.

28 Istanbul which lies at the exit from the Black Sea to the Mediterranean.

29 A cold water current from the Antarctic which flows up the western coast of South America.

30 An early form of sextant used for the observation of heavenly bodies. Having a smaller arc, it measures a lesser angle than the sextant, eg 45°.

31 Shrouds are the ropes or wires holding up and taking the sideways strain on a mast. The stays hold the mast fore and aft.

32 The slang name for the red ensign.

33 In a flashing light the flashes are of short duration compared to the dark period.
In an occulating light, the light periods predominate.

34 He was in distress and needed urgent assistance.

35 · · · — — · · ·

36 The futtock shrouds.

37 Spilling (the wind from the sail).

38 An old method of fastening planks to frames in a ship with the use of strong wooden pins. (From 'tree nails'.)

39 Wooden or metal projections pointing forward of a yacht's mast as distinct from crosstrees which project sideways.

40 The quarantine flag.

41 A type of power yacht developed by Bertram, planing successfully at the expense of power but claiming improved performance in rough water.

42 They are makers of marine diesel engines.

43 Propeller efficiency is greater at low speeds. An engine produces more power at high speeds. A reduction gear reduces engine speed to the propeller shaft.

44 A diesel engine in which the spray of fuel is injected into an ante-chamber rather than into the cylinder direct.

45 (a) Cruising Club of America.
   (b) Ocean Sailing Club.
   (c) Royal Institution of Naval Architects.
   (d) Royal Naval Sailing Association.
46 The shortest path between two points on the earth's surface.
47 Whale.
48 The sun.
49 Commander D. A. Rayner. Among his writings were *The Enemy Below* and *Escort.*
50 Drunk!
51 In 1952, to the US liner, *United States.*
52 The open dory in which Chay Blyth, assisted by fellow soldier in the Parachute Regiment, Captain John Ridgeway, rowed the Atlantic from Cape Cod to the Aran Islands in 1966. The trip took them ninety-two days.
53 Set up by Act of Parliament in 1714, during the reign of Queen Anne, this was the name commonly used for the Commissioners for the Discovery of Longitude at Sea.
54 One in which a yacht is chartered without a crew and with a minimum of restrictions as to her use by the charterer.
55 A small boat used for the carrying of provisions (vegetables, fruit etc) to ships lying in harbour.
56 A merchant ship fitted in World War II with a catapult with which a fighter aircraft could be launched to protect a convoy from air attack. The name derived from the initial letters – Catapult Aircraft Merchant Ship.
57 Cape Finisterre.
58 The French navigator, Jacques Cartier (1491–1557).
59 A crance (crans or cranze) iron.
60 An anchor, in sailor's slang.
61 A benevolent fund for the navy established by Sir Francis Drake, Lord Howard of Effingham and Sir John Hawkins in 1590. Seamen paid 6d a month into it for the benefit of the wounded and the widows of those killed in action.
62 A violent easterly squall of which mariners must beware when sailing off the western coast of Nicaragua.
63 It was one of a group of islands, over 600 miles south of Tokyo, which was of vital importance to the Japanese. It served as a staging post for Japanese aircraft flying to the Philippines and the South Pacific.

64 The top part of the barrel of a capstan, incorporating square slots for the capstan bars, inserted for the raising of the anchor. The operation of weighing anchor by hand is now, of course, virtually a thing of the past.

65 The Portuguese navigator, Vasco da Gama (c 1460–1524).

66 The *Henri Grâce à Dieu*, also known as the *Great Harry*.

67 Thor Heyerdahl, to cross the Atlantic in the type of vessel the ancient Egyptians used. Both vessels were constructed of papyrus reeds, but the first *Ra* – named after the sun god of ancient Egypt – disintegrated in heavy seas near the West Indies.

In 1970, Heyerdahl successfully crossed in *Ra II* from Safi, Morocco, to Bridgetown, Barbados, and so demonstrated that such voyages by the early Egyptians were within the bounds of possibility.

68 The dreadnought battleship, HMS *Iron Duke*.

69 *Hoshi* is the gaff schooner owned and sailed by the Island Cruising Club based at Salcombe, Devon. *Provident* is the traditional Brixham sailing trawler owned by the Maritime Trust and sailed by the Island Cruising Club.

70 Eric Tabarly, the noted single-hander who had five yachts of that name. (He won many famous ocean races in them.)

71 In the early 1930s, Hitler ordered the German Department of Labour to set up an organisation to replace the trade unions. This became known as the 'Strength Through Joy' organisation, and it was compulsory for all factory workers to join.

Through German shipping lines, a maritime branch was formed to enable workers to enjoy cruises during their annual holidays. Ships were allocated for the purpose.

72 At the time of writing Sir Peter Parker is chairman of British Rail. An Admiral of the Fleet, Sir Peter Parker (1721–1811), was a close friend and patron of Nelson when the latter was serving as a young captain in the West Indies.

73 0°.

74 In sailor's lingo the pooling of the financial resources of a group of seamen for the buying of liquor or for a run ashore.

75 Built in great secrecy by the Japanese, they were sister ships and at 65,000 tons displacement were the biggest battleships ever built.

They were both sunk by the Americans towards the end of World War II; in the case of the *Yamato* not before she had been hit by ten torpedoes and twenty-three bombs. It took twenty torpedoes and thirty-three bombs to despatch the *Musashi.*